Church and Society in the Late Twentieth Century:
The Economic and Political Task

RONALD H. PRESTON

Church and Society
in the Late
Twentieth Century:
The Economic and Political Task

The Scott Holland Lectures for 1983

SCM PRESS LTD

334 01943 5

First published 1983
by SCM Press Ltd
26–30 Tottenham Road
London N1 4BZ

Typeset by Gloucester Typesetting Services
Printed in Great Britain by
Billings & Son Ltd,
London and Worcester

In gratitude for the Professors and Lecturers of the
London School of Economics 1932–5,
whose reasoned disagreements among themselves
within a shared concern for human welfare
gave their students an education of the highest quality;
and in particular a tribute to
the memory of Professor R. H. Tawney,
the first Scott Holland lecturer.

The Scott Holland Memorial Lectures

on 'The Religion of the Incarnation in its bearing on the social and economic life of man', held in memory of Henry Scott Holland, Canon of St Paul's Cathedral, 1884–1910 and Regius Professor of Divinity in the University of Oxford, 1910–18.

Contents

Contents

Preface

This is a revision and expansion of the 1983 Scott Holland lectures. It represents in many respect a continued reflection on the theme of my Maurice lectures on 'Religion and the Persistence of Capitalism' (1977), a theme which has been one of my main preoccupations for many years. There was an intermediate state between the two series of lectures. A consultation was held in Manchester, for which the Maurice lectures served as a kind of 'position' paper, and in relation to which other papers were written. All these were subsequently revised and published in *Christians and the Future of Social Democracy* edited by M. H. Taylor, 1982; mine became an opening chapter on 'Capitalism, Democracy and Christianity'.

Further reflection would have been necessary in any case because of several new factors. (1) The economic recession proved deeper and more prolonged than I expected. Indeed no analyst forecast how severe and long would be the post-1973 OPEC inflationary slump. Comparing the years 1973–1983 with the previous decade 1963–1973, our growth ratio has been cut by one third and the rate of inflation and the number of unemployed doubled. (2) There has been a marked growth in what may be termed a 'radical right' philosophy, which was echoed theologically in E. R. Norman's BBC Reith Lectures of 1978, 'Christianity and the World Order'. It is significant that it was the first explicitly Christian theme in the series of Reith Lectures, and caused far more discussion than most of them. The discussion is still smouldering. (3) The serious floundering on economic issues of our two main political parties has been alarming. The fact that they have represented adversary politics at their worst has provoked the birth of the Social Democratic Party and the SDP-Liberal alliance. This has led much Christian opinion in reaction to accept too easily its

9

underplaying of conflicts of interest, and the adversarial element in politics that results from it. (4) The increasing accuracy and relative cheapness of small-scale nuclear weapons has made the chances of the escalation of a nuclear conflict more probable and the world a much more dangerous place.

These factors have not caused me to modify the basic stance of the Maurice lectures, but they have sharpened thought, and made me think more strongly that an advanced industrial society has some searching adaptations of policies and institutions to make fairly quickly, and that the philosophy of possessive individualism espoused by the 'radical right' is a false basis on which to act.

The first chapter is a revised version of a paper prepared for one of two private consultations in Vancouver in 1982. The first was on 'Religion, Economics and Social Thought', and the second on 'The Morality of the Market'. They were arranged by the Fraser Institute of that city and financed by the Liberty Fund of Indianapolis, USA. Both are dedicated to promoting the free capitalist market economy. The Fraser Institute has created a Centre for the Study of Economics and Religion. This was the first time it had had a consultation with theologians on economic issues. Most participants came from North America and were professional economists and most were Christians, though there were also present some notable adherents of other faiths. Most shared the outlook of the Fraser Institute, but there was complete freedom of expression and genuine dialogue. If at times I found myself listening to hoary fallacies which I had thought disposed of when I was an undergraduate, at others I found valuable material being presented which influenced me in the Scott Holland lectures, and for which I am grateful, as I am to the Fraser Institute for the invitation to be present. The fact that the first chapter was originally prepared for this non-English constituency has influenced the presentation.

The second chapter is a considerably altered version of a public lecture originally given at Lakehead University, Thunder Bay, Ontario in 1981. A substantive part of the book was also given as the Moorhouse lectures at Melbourne University in August 1983, and as the Marshall Memorial lecture at Trinity College there in the same month. Some of the material was also given in University centres in New Zealand in the previous month. The second Appendix is a more detailed treatment of an issue closely related to the lectures which I have thought for some time needed a fresh exploration. I read it to the Staff Seminar of the Department of Social and Pastoral Theology in Manchester University, and I am grateful to my successor, Professor Anthony Dyson, for adding to his kindnesses by giving me the opportunity to benefit from criticism.

The theme is obviously a wide one. If the first part of the title were adequately to be covered a great deal more social, sociological and cultural analysis of society and of the churches would be required; the second part of the title indicates that I have confined myself to basic economic issues and the way they lead to political ones, and I have concentrated on the position of those advanced industrial societies which are heirs of the Judaeo-Christian and the Classical tradition. Similarly a full bibliography would be vast; but the ones I have provided should give anyone a start on most themes, and one book will then easily lead to others. I have excluded books published before 1900 and, for reasons of space, those mentioned in the notes. References to relevant articles will be found in the notes, where some points are taken further than the lectures allowed.

I am conscious of many whose thoughts have influenced me, and there must be many of whom I am unconscious; but of personal influences there are three whom out of gratitude I must mention. As I had the privilege as an undergraduate of being a student of R. H. Tawney, and kept in touch with him until he died, I felt particularly honoured to be asked to give lectures in a series which he inaugurated. William Temple was an inspiration to many of my generation. I end by asking, Who are the heirs of Tawney and Temple? If I had gone beyond this country I should have added a third name, that of Reinhold Niebuhr. What all three basically stood for needs bringing to bear on the new situation of late twentieth-century advanced industrial societies.

It remains to thank the Dean and Canons of Manchester Cathedral for allowing me to give the lectures in a building with which I have had so many happy associations since 1957; and those who heard and commented on the lectures, which has helped in the process of revision. It is a pleasure also to thank the Revd Canon Dr John Gaden and his colleagues at Trinity College, Melbourne; the Very Revd David Coles of Napier, a former research student, who arranged my visit to New Zealand; Miss Margaret Lydamore and the staff of the SCM Press; Mrs Brenda Peck, Secretary in the Department of Social and Pastoral Theology in the University of Manchester and Mrs Kathleen Sheehan, Secretary to the William Temple Foundation, Manchester, for typing the manuscript under pressure. My wife, Mary, is a rock of stability and over the years has made possible far more than she knows; a tribute to her must be included, inadequate as it inevitably is.

Manchester,   Ronald Preston
St Gregory the Great
3 September 1983

I

The Legacy of the Christian Socialist Movement
in England

There are many different understandings of socialism. In 1924 Angelo Rappoport referred to thirty nine definitions of it, and in 1975 R. N. Berki found four major tendencies, in different proportions, in major socialist theories.[1] These four are: (1) Egalitarianism and Communitarianism; (2) a Christian moralism of high ideals; (3) a Rationalism, deriving from the Enlightenment, involving expertise and a meritocracy; (4) a Libertarian and Romantic strain of an individualistic, and partly anarchic, type. The second element receives scanty treatment in Berki's book – too scanty – but at least his analysis warns us against exaggerating the legacy of the Christian Socialist movement to socialism. It may well be that it had more, if diffused, influence on the churches. Berki in fact refers only to St Paul at Phil. 2.3f. 'Do nothing from selfishness or conceit, but in humility count others better than yourselves. Let each of you look not only to his own interests, but also to the interests of others' (RSV), and to Thomas More's *Utopia* of 1516. I have never before seen the Philippians passage mentioned in this connection. To Berki those of whom I am now writing might never have existed. Nor is it clear what precisely the term 'moralism' means to him. He confines himself to saying that for Christian moralism the chief values are 'social justice, peace, co-operation, and brotherhood'; and that for it 'Capitalism is a fundamentally unjust system of society'; it is 'cruel and inhuman in that it sets man against man, extolling selfishness and mutual enmity in the guise of "free competition" '.[2] We shall look more closely at this judgment in due course.

What was it that made Morgan Phillips say a generation ago, when he was Secretary of the Labour Party, that the Labour movement owed more to Methodism than to Marx? The Labour Party is the product of three movements; the co-operative movement, the trade unions, and the Independent Labour Party. Phillips was referring in a succinct sentence to the large number of pioneers in all three who came from a Christian background. Most of them were Primitive (not United or Wesleyan) Methodists, or Baptists. Many of them in the days before a national educational system was established, learned to read and write in a Sunday school, and even into the twentieth century it was in a Sunday Bible class where they learned to speak in public. They carried this Christian background, sometimes considerably diluted into an ethical humanism, into the Labour movement.[3] This was not due to the policy of the central organs of the denominations, far from it, but to the ethos of some local congregations. The result is that there was a different ethos about the Labour movement in Britain from that of the social democratic parties on the continent of Europe, such as the French or German socialist parties. They did not easily understand one another. The continentals tended to talk in the language of a bowdlerized Marxism and the British in that of an ethical idealism with Christian undertones. This situation is now practically dead; an ideological vacuum is left, as neither language retains its power. The Christian concepts faded because the Christian churches never succeeded in maintaining sufficient links with working-class life to maintain them. For a brief period there were Labour churches, pioneered by John Trevor of Upper Brook Street Unitarian church in Manchester in 1891. They grew rapidly in the 1890s, mostly in Lancashire and the West Riding of Yorkshire, but to a lesser extent in other major industrial areas. At one time there were about fifty. Most had faded away by 1914, and the remaining few shortly after 1918. The members were mainly drawn from young working-class men and women under forty who had been influenced by, but had drifted away from, evangelical Free church religion, although retaining a diffused Christian outlook. Some moved back into the mainstream churches as these began to show more awareness of a 'social gospel'; the majority became more exclusively political, and the theological content of the Labour churches became lost in their socialism. Their story has never adequately been told.[4] Neither has that of some of the more recent Christian socialist groups which I shall mention in the second main section of this chapter. In it I shall on occasion have to stray beyond strictly socialist into more general Christian social movements, but the emphasis is definitely on the former. Adequately to deal with the latter would be a very large task requiring a book to itself.

1. The Christian Socialist Movement 1848–54

The Christian Socialist Movement, as it is usually thought of, antedates these pioneering activities in the Labour movement. The Movement's origin can be precisely dated to the evening of 10 April 1848. That afternoon the large Chartist march to Parliament from Kennington Common in south London had dissolved in a rainstorm. In the evening J. M. Ludlow, who had been in Paris in February at the uprising which overthrew Louis Philippe, met with Charles Kingsley in F. D. Maurice's house. They stayed up till 4.0 a.m. on 11 April writing a manifesto 'To the Workmen of England', urging Chartists to join those who favoured non-violent reform and signed 'A Working Parson'. The Chartist movement was not in fact violent in its aims or methods and, indeed, everything it worked for has been achieved except annual Parliaments. However the manifesto sought to turn Chartists away from demands for political and economic reform (its whole tone seems condescending), and it was not until 1850 that Frederick Denison Maurice and his friends used the term socialist. It was a comparatively new word which had come to be used in the period of intense political and economic argument and social change after the Napoleonic wars,[5] appearing in print in English for the first time in the Owenist *Co-operative Magazine* of November 1827. Because of its Owenite origin it was associated with atheism, whereas Communism at this time had strong religious overtones. All the bolder, therefore, of the Christian socialists to use it as, to quote Maurice, they sought to influence 'the unsocial Christians and the unChristian socialists'.[6]

The Christian Socialist Movement was important because it meant a recovery of a theological critique of the assumptions behind the social order which had died out with the collapse of traditional Anglican and Puritan moral theology at the end of the seventeenth century. From the time of the early Fathers, Christian theology had included such a critique, though it is scarcely found in the New Testament, chiefly because of the expectation of an imminent *parousia* or return of Christ. Anglicans and Puritans continued the tradition after the Reformation, the last notable exponent being Richard Baxter, an ecumenical church leader before his time, and an Independent minister at Kidderminster in Worcestershire.[7] The tradition probably died out because the dynamic forces of merchant capitalism and later industrial capitalism were too much for a Christian social theology which was too tied in its assumptions to a static society. However the effect of the absence of one can be seen in John Wesley. He attacked particular abuses, and instigated some voluntary social improvement efforts, but his social theology was merely individualism writ large.[8] So it came about that the social and economic upheavals which we call the Industrial Revolution produced among Christians some inchoate protests and some nostalgic wishes for a past situation, but no theological critique, and that at a time when an atomistic social and economic theory was being treated as a law of God. The Christian Socialist Movement lasted only from 1848 to 1854, was unsuccessful in its practical experiments and unformed in its theories, but it did go to the root of the matter in this fundamental point, as we shall see.

The leaders were a diverse group. J. M. Ludlow had lived in Paris, and been open to the ideas of Saint-Simon, Blanc and Fourier.[9] Some of Blanc's social workshops (*ateliers nationaux*) had been set up in Paris in 1848, and all failed. To a lesser extent he was influenced also by the early English socialists like Robert Owen. However he was a staunch Anglican, and the doctrine of the incarnation was more decisive for him than any of these sources. Charles Kingsley was an upper class Burkeian gentleman-parson with a paternalistic concern for the working conditions of the poor, of which he acquired some knowledge. He it was who, before Marx, said that the Bible had been used as a book for the rich to keep the poor in order.[10] But he had few constructive ideas. E. V. Neale was a wealthy latitudinarian Christian, primarily interested in co-operation. It was his money that financed the producers' co-operatives which the Christian socialists set up from February 1850, for tailors, builders, shoemakers, bakers and others.[11] They had failed by 1854, or soon after, because of quarrels with the managers, dishonesties, or the individualism of

16

the workers.[12] It was these disasters that led the Christian socialists to the too easy – and Pelagian – conclusion that middle-class people often came to, that the workers needed to be educated before they would be fit to govern themselves. However Ludlow and Neale turned to give practical help to the burgeoning Labour movement, in Friendly Societies and in the co-operative movement.[13] There was in fact early legislative fruit from their activities in the Industrial and Provident Societies Act of 1852 which, among other things, gave legal security to producers' co-operatives, though with unlimited liability. It was F. D. Maurice who was to turn particularly to education in founding the Working Men's College in Camden Town.

Everyone has agreed at the time and since that F. D. Maurice[14] was the leader, and that for him his theology is the key to all he did. From his Unitarian upbringing onwards Maurice is the archetype of the theologian who endeavours to hold together the many sided mysteries of life in one comprehensive overview. In his intellectual formation he absorbed influences from Julius Hare, his tutor at Cambridge, S. T. Coleridge, Erskine of Linlathen, Edward Irving, and many others, but by 1838 he had reached what in most respects was his permanent position in the best known of his voluminous writings, *The Kingdom of Christ*. He had no sympathy for the kind of socialism advocated by the early English and French 'socialists', and indeed was suspicious of all organizations for concrete change, so it was uncharacteristic of him both to advocate the use of the term socialist in 1850 and to support the setting up of working men's associations, of which the tailors were the first, in the same year. His general position was that social change must be achieved by religious means. Hence the churches must be induced to look outwards because Christ has redeemed *all* men, and his new order is already in being whether they realize it or not. The infinite love of God and the Lordship of Christ, not human sin, are the starting points of Christian theology. Christ has redeemed men in and for community with one another in God. Men seek to possess for themselves what they can only have in a community of giving and receiving. Maurice resisted all attempts to narrow the thought or boundaries of the church. It was to him the equivalent of the kingdom of God. Theology harmonizes the truth in every school or system of thought. He was a leading example of one who holds that men are usually right in what they affirm and wrong in what they deny. To him socialism meant the principle of co-operation in society. The various classes, monarchy, aristocracy, and trading, must carry out their function for the benefit of all; but a fourth estate of the workers is needed and they must be educated to co-operate harmoniously with the other estates. Long established institutions, such as the monarchy or the aristocracy, are divinely intended, and social reform must be an organic growth. The *Christian* socialist's task is to declare a universal moral order of fellowship (which *secular* socialists want to build) to exist already.

Much of this does not seem very far from Disraeli's *Sybil*. Could he equally well have talked of Christian toryism? Was he a progressive conservative? It is tempting to think so. However toryism is partly made up of a hierarchical view of society with a stress on the duty of the higher orders of society to care for and uplift the lower orders, and partly of another increasingly prominent element, laissez-faire liberalism, which stands at least in theory for competition and a free market as the basis of the economic order and such social order as it is necessary for the state to organize. To this Maurice was entirely opposed. By the middle of the nineteenth century the ideology of laissez-faire was dominant. The theory of the free market had had ideological overtones from the time of its classic adumbration by Adam Smith, taking to itself elements from Hobbes and Locke, some Christian insights derived by several removes from certain strains in Calvinism and, more recently, influenced by utilitarian philosophy. Its over-all interpretation of life can be called a philosophy of 'possessive individualism'.[15] Many Christians regarded what they called the laws of economics as the laws of God, in the sense of the laws of the Newtonian universe. This is expressed in two lines from the eighteenth century hymn:

> Laws, which never shall be broken
> For their guidance He hath made.

The laws of supply and demand are akin to the law that fire burns. This was expressed particularly clearly in some nonconformist circles, though it was widely held by Anglicans too. The Congregational journal, *The British Quarterly Review*, for instance, declared in 1846 that 'Economical truth is no less divine than astronomical truth. The laws which govern the phenomenon of production and exchange are as truly laws of God as those which govern day and night.'[16] It was to this view that Maurice was implacably opposed. He wrote to Kingsley on 2 January 1850: 'Competition is put forth as a law of the universe. This is a lie. The time has come for us to declare that it is a lie by word and deed. I see no way but associating for work instead of strikes.'[17] And in the first of the eight *Tracts on Christian Socialism*, later in the year, he says on the first page: 'Anyone who recognizes the principle of co-operation as a stronger and truer principle than that of competition has the right to the honour and disgrace of being called a socialist.' It is here that the legacy of Christian socialism lies. The philosophy of possessive individualism, which has had a renewal in recent years both in the UK and the USA, is less and less appropriate to an advanced industrial society.[18] Moreover it is an unchristian view. True, it has some emphases which are congenial to Christianity, a stress on personal responsibility for instance, but these are outweighed by the falseness of its overall view of life. This ignores the fact that the structures of society are prior to the individuality of persons and affect their formation profoundly, for good or ill, from infancy. In the Christian view men and women are meant to live in communities of mutual giving and receiving, and not to try to be as independent of everyone else as possible.

How this is to be expressed in social and economic institutions is a major question, and capitalism may well have developed some, such as the free market, which it would be folly to throw away altogether. Maurice had no grasp of the fundamentals of an economic policy, nor of the details, nor did the group get far with them in these years. Their writings are full of vague and imprecise reflections on a wide range of issues – trade unions, education, health legislation, the renewal of village life, the reform of the House of Lords – and many more. But they did not hark back to a pre-industrial Britain. Maurice, however, soon split with Ludlow on the issue of political democracy, and they went their different ways, though maintaining contact. A certain mystery remains as to why the others agreed when Maurice turned to education in 1853–4 and the projects were handed over to the co-operative industrial and commercial union. Ludlow refused to take on the leadership and wrote in his *Autobiography*: 'Maurice is better and wiser than all of us put together and we had better follow him.' Yet he was in two minds on the matter, for he was also severely critical of Maurice. It was consistent with Maurice's theology to hold that only Christianity could bring about the kind of society he sought, but his unwillingness to operate with others on the level of justice is no model for us.

Some of the Christian socialists tended to favour producers' co-operation too simply. They saw it as a way of securing co-operation instead of competition in the processes of production, as well as a means of educating the workers. It remains one serious alternative system of production, which has been chiefly successful in agriculture. But it does not solve all problems. It forgets that producers of goods or services have themselves a vested interest, an entirely proper one which needs the power of organization and representation behind it, but which also needs balancing by the organized power of the vested interests of consumers. For the rest the Christian socialists' wider and subsequent activities in almost all the pioneering social developments in Victorian England provide excellent examples of how Christian insights can be, and need to be, built into the structures of social and economic life, where Christians are operating with their fellow citizens of different faiths or none. Together they need to make these structures operate in better and more human ways, and to devise new ones. An enormous amount of sheer hard work was contributed by the Christian socialists to Victorian society, even though Maurice himself had drawn back. Intellectually they were to have, after a pause, a long lasting effect, partly on a series of small groups, partly a diffused influence on the church at large, and partly on a few outstanding leaders. Some of this story has often been told, but not that of the recent past. It is to these aspects that I now turn.

2. Christian socialist groups from 1877 to 1980

The pause was occasioned by the years of greatest Victorian self-confidence, heralded by the Great Exhibition of 1851. Later in the century things changed. 1877 saw the foundation of the Guild of St Matthew by Stewart Headlam, with Thomas Hancock as its leading thinker; both were Anglican priests. Its aim was to 'study social and political questions in the light of the incarnation', and to stress the 'social significance of the sacrament of the eucharist'. It claimed the influence of Maurice, though in practical terms it interpreted his thinking differently, not seeing co-operative production but the state as a 'sacred' organ of reform. There is probably some influence of Oxford Hegelianism here. Headlam agreed with the Fabians on the role of the state. He was a member of the executive of the Fabian Society, and in 1892 gave a lecture on 'Christian Socialism' which was published as a Fabian Tract 42. By 1899 the influence of the Guild was lost, though it continued until 1910. Part of the loss of influence was due to its advocacy of Henry George's Single Tax (on land values) which George had propagated in a tour of Britain in 1885. Headlam was also a child of his time in regarding the kingdom of God as something we are to work towards building on earth, an idea common among liberal Protestants which also influenced Catholic-minded Anglicans. The journal of the Guild, *The Church Reformer*, was good, and its influence was considerable when it is realized that at its peak in 1894–5 its membership was not more than four hundred. At bottom it was élitist, as was shown by its opposition to the formation of the Independent Labour Party.[19]

Beside the Guild of St Matthew there was another group, led by J. L. Joynes and H. H. Champion, who began in 1883 to issue a paper called *The Christian Socialist*, influenced by both Stewart Headlam and Henry George. The Guild was too Anglican for them. In 1886 their paper became the organ of an inter-denominational Christian Socialist Society, which had faded by 1892. However in 1894 another inter-denominational body, the Christian Socialist League, was founded with the prominent Baptist minister Dr John Clifford as president. It only lasted four years. The Quakers also had a society akin to the Guild, the Socialist Quaker Society, which lasted from 1898 to 1919. It published *Ploughshare* as its journal and S. G. Hobson was one of its leading figures.

1889 was an important year. It saw the London dock strike, the publication of *Fabian Essays*, and the Catholic Anglican essays *Lux Mundi*, and also the founding of the Christian Social Union. This was definitely not a socialist movement, but because of its debt to Maurice and the influence of some of its members who were socialists it must be mentioned. Bishop Westcott of Durham was the first president and Henry Scott Holland the chairman. Westcott's social thought was inclined to be cloudy. At times he would appear to be saying that the extension of family love would be the means to sweeten structurally unchanged social class relationships. The CSU, like Kingsley, campaigned against sweated industries, especially in the tailoring trade. It organized a Sweated Industries Exhibition in 1907, and influenced the Trade Boards Act of 1909 which produced machinery for setting minimum wages in industries where the workers were too scattered and poor to be easily organized in trade unions. The journal of the CSU, *Commonwealth*, was edited by Scott Holland from 1897 to his death in 1918. Two years later the CSU joined with the Navvy Mission to form the Industrial Christian Fellowship, with Studdert Kennedy ('Woodbine Willie' of the First World War) as its prophet. It still exists in a minor way. The CSU did not achieve much after 1909, though in comparison with other groups we are concerned with it had a much larger membership, about six thousand at its maximum, including quite a number of bishops. It was purely Anglican. And it had no working-class or trade union members. The Quakers had a parallel body to the CSU from 1904, the Friends' Social Union, with Seebohm Rowntree and George Cadbury among its members.

It was this lack of working-class contacts, together with the flurry of excitement after the 1906 election which saw the landslide to the Liberals and the arrival of fifty-three Labour Members of Parliament, that led in that year to the foundation of the first Anglican society specifically committed to socialism, the Church Socialist League. It was much less London-centred than most of what I have been describing, with many church radicals from the north of England as members. Conrad Noel was its paid organizer. The socialism it favoured was Guild socialism, which by then was being discussed in some sections of the Labour movement as an alternative to the wage system. There would be a Guild for each industry, each member would have the same status and the division between employer and employee would be overcome. The CSL also continued the preference of Maurice and most of his friends for producers' co-operatives. At its peak in 1912 it had about one thousand

members. The Socialist Quaker Society was also attracted to
Guild socialism. Once again there was a Nonconformist parallel
to an Anglican society, the Free Church Socialist League,
founded in 1909. Philip Snowden, who was to be the first Labour
Chancellor of the Exchequer in 1924, was a member. It soon
faded. The first Free Church book on socialism came from the
Wesleyan Methodist minister S. E. Keeble in 1907, *Industrial
Daydreams*. He was to live to write *Christian Responsibility for the
Social Order* in 1922, and play a considerable part in the COPEC
Conference of 1924.[20]

In 1916 Conrad Noel split from the CSL to form the Catholic
Crusade on the basis of 'the fatherhood of God, the brotherhood
of man, and the sacramental principle', another interesting
example of Catholic Anglicans being influenced by liberal
Protestantism, with whom Noel shared the idea of building the
kingdom of God. The Catholic Crusade had a libertarian strain
going back to John Ball, and much more recently to William
Morris and Peter Kropotkin. It welcomed the Russian revolution
of 1917, and then itself split after Stalin had ousted Trotsky.
Those who supported Trotsky formed the Order of the Church
Militant. The Catholic Crusade was disbanded in 1936 and the
Order of the Church Militant continued until Noel's death in
1942. A theological weakness is revealed in the lack of political
judgment in evaluating the Soviet Union. The same defect was
to be revealed by Hewlett Johnson, the 'Red' Dean of Canterbury
in his speeches and writings, and in a secularized form by Sidney
and Beatrice Webb. In no case was it due to a slavish following
of Marxist theory.[21]

The remaining members of the CSL split again in 1924.
Another section of High Church Anglicans formed the League of
the kingdom of God to seek a 'specifically Christian sociology'.
It became closely associated with and effectively replaced by an
annual Anglo-Catholic Summer School of Sociology ('Christian'
sociology) which took place from 1925 for nearly forty years.
V. A. Demant was its leading thinker. Behind it was the Christendom Trust, largely financed by Maurice Reckitt, which published the journal *Christendom* from 1931 to 1950 under his
editorship. An early book *The Return of Christendom* in 1922
foreshadowed it, and another *Prospect for Christendom* (1945) was
a herald of its downfall. In its desire for a distinctive social

theology it distanced itself from all that was going on, indeed from all social reality. It is too simple to say that it hankered after a return to the Middle Ages, but the mediaeval strain in its thought led it to advocate a return from industrialism to rural life, the reversal of urbanization and even barter rather than a financial system. It liked neither capitalism nor the adumbrations of the Welfare State under the Attlee government of 1945, nor state socialism, but wanted something different and distinctively Christian. It was vague as to the 'natural' order to which we should return, and was perhaps rather more informed on cultural than economic and political issues. For a time its leaders advocated the Social Credit scheme of the engineer Major C. H. Douglas (as did Hewlett Johnson), which is based on a simple economic fallacy.[22] Its activities were absorbed by the Industrial Christian Fellowship in 1957. The Christendom Trust was refounded on a new basis in 1971.

The other section of the Church Socialist League became in 1924 the Society of Socialist Christians, changing its name in 1931 to the Socialist Christian League and from being Anglican to becoming interdenominational. It, too, talked of building the kingdom of God on earth and of the sacramental principle. It generated some activity in local groups, notably in Stepney in the East End of London by John Groser, an Anglican priest who became widely known throughout the country, and it had a number of MPs as members, including George Lansbury who was for a time leader of the Labour Party. It continued until a re-grouping of socialist Christian forces in 1960.[23]

The 1930s was a decade of economic recession, the growth of Fascism and the rise of Nazism, and deepening international crisis. It was the time of the influential Left Book Club. There grew up under the same influences a group of Christian socialists called the Christian Left. It contained a number of academics, of whom the best known was the philosopher John Macmurray. This was the first group not at all in the Maurice tradition. It took Marxism seriously in its philosophy and social analysis, unlike Conrad Noel and his associates. Indeed it accepted the Marxist criticism of religion as spuriously idealistic and affirmed much of what Marxism affirms but insisted that Jesus saw it first.[24] The Christian Left hardly survived the Stalin-Hitler pact. In this same decade there was an informal group, mainly made up of several members of the staff and senior friends of the Student Christian Movement who were influenced by Reinhold Niebuhr, and who believed with him that it was necessary to move to the right theologically and to the left politically. That is to say to reject the utopianism of much of both liberal Protestantism and liberal Catholicism with regard to the building of the kingdom of God, and to take a socialist political position on the basis of what seemed the most cogent social and political analysis of the events of the decade, an analysis which nevertheless was not Marxist. Knowledge of the work of New Testament scholars on the nature of the kingdom of God in the ministry of Jesus was a key factor in this position.[25]

Then came the war. In the middle of it William Temple, who had been Archbishop of York since 1929, called a conference in 1941 at Malvern on 'The Life of the Church and the Order of Society'. It was a confuscd affair.[26] Those on the political left tried to get a resolution passed to the effect that the private ownership of the principal industrial resources of the community is a stumbling block which makes it harder for men to live Christian lives. But they could only get agreement to the phrase '*may be* a stumbling block'. So next year they formed the Council of Clergy and Ministers for Common Ownership, with Bishop Blunt of Bradford as president and Sir Richard Acland and Sir Stafford Cripps as influential members. The Bishop resigned in 1947 because of its uncritical support of the Soviet Union (thus re-calling the Catholic Crusade, the Order of the Church Militant and the Christian Left), and was succeeded by Hewlett Johnson. In 1952 it changed its name to the Society of Socialist Clergy and Ministers, and in 1960 merged into a new socialist Christian group, including the Socialist Christian League, after discussing for some time with it the proper attitude to the USSR.[27] Out of these discussions came a pamphlet in 1959 *Papers from The Lamb*, and on its basis the new movement was called the Christian Socialist Movement, with the veteran Methodist minister, Dr Donald Soper (later to become a Peer), as chairman.[28] Its journal was first called *The Christian Socialist Movement News* and later *The Christian Socialist*; it continues to be published. The Movement has about nine hundred members, including some MPs.

There had been a Roman Catholic Social Guild since 1909

(like the Christian Social Union), which published *The Catholic Worker* and established Plater College at Oxford, a counterpart to Ruskin College, but it was not socialist. In the mid-1960s a Roman Catholic semi-Marxist group, Slant, flourished briefly. The impetus was given by the opening provided by Pope John XXIII to a more constructive attitude to Marxism instead of the previous total opposition. Hitherto Roman Catholics had played little part in Christian socialist movements (as distinct from the Labour movement) largely because of the condemnation of socialism in papal teaching from the pioneer social Encyclical *Rerum Novarum* in 1891. As to Marxism, John XXIII deftly modified the previous blanket condemnation by these artless words in the Encyclical *Pacem in Terris* of 1963. 'Who can deny that these movements (*sc.* false philosophical teaching regarding the nature, origin and destiny of man and the universe) in so far as they conform to the dictates of right reason and are interpreters of the lawful aspirations of the human person, contain elements that are positive and deserving of approval?' These words were a prelude to a new *Ostpolitik* on the part of the Vatican.[29] The Slant Manifesto was published in 1966. In the next decade the Christians for Socialism group took its place, influenced by Latin American liberation theology with its Marxist tones, but it does not flourish.

The year 1975 saw three initiatives. A Quaker Socialist Society re-started, with about two hundred and fifty members; there was the launching among Anglican Catholics of the Jubilee Group, a society reviving in terms of the late twentieth century the concerns of the Guild of St Matthew, the League of the Kingdom of God and the Catholic Crusade; and in reaction to the inadequacies of the Call to the Nation of the two Anglican Archbishops, a group called Christians for Socialism began to meet, based on Manchester. Its energies have chiefly gone into a bi-monthly journal *Christian Statesman* (a title modelled on the left wing weekly *New Statesman*), which has a circulation of about one thousand. In 1980 these groups and a number of others, twenty-one in all, of varying degrees of radicalism began to collaborate in a loose organization, COSPEC (Christian Organizations for Social, Political and Economic Change). Indirectly related to this a symposium, *Agenda for Prophets*, appeared in that year.[30]

After this survey of a hundred years of small Christian socialist groups there are three men to whom it is well to refer specifically. The first is Bishop Charles Gore.[31] He was the biggest troubler of the Church of England establishment because he would not let awkward questions be passed by. He was a radical social reformer rather than a socialist, though he produced a sympathetic lecture on Christianity and Socialism to the Pan-Anglican Congress of 1908. In 1913 he edited a symposium *Property, its Duties and Rights*, which remains a fundamental treatment of Christian teaching on property. Gore was alert to the moral perils of wealth, especially the idleness of the rich, and agreed with Roman Catholic teaching in regarding a living wage as the first charge on industry.

William Temple as a young man in 1908 wrote a celebrated article in *The Economic Review*[32] which covers many of the standard themes of Christian socialists. He is commenting on Eph. 4.11ff., the passage which deals with the varying gifts which Christ gives to Christians in the church for each to use for the building up of the others, so that all achieve together their full maturity. He says it articulates the fullest 'scheme of evolutionary socialism, so far as all fundamental points are concerned, that has yet been achieved by man'. He goes on to say that the church must be concerned with the material world because (1) the doctrine of the incarnation means that Spirit demands bodily expression, (2) Jesus healed without enquiring into the spiritual attitude of sufferers, (3) the church owns property and employs persons. The church needs the Labour movement, and the Labour movement needs the church for its inspiration and rituals. There is the need to replace the competitive basis of society by a co-operative basis, for competition is inherently a spirit of selfishness, even of hatred. It is the interest of every man against his fellows. 'There is no middle path between the acceptance of socialism and the declaration that the Gospel cannot be applied to economics. The alternative stands before us – socialism or heresy; we are involved in one or the other.' In 1918 he joined the Labour Party and left it some time between 1921 and 1925 (it is not clear when or precisely why). At the end of his life, however, in *Christianity and Social Order* he said 'I do not simply advocate socialism or common ownership', and writes of the necessity to get the best out of socialism and individualism.[33]

R. H. Tawney was both a similar and a different figure. He was similar in that his social, educational and theological formation was like that of Gore and Temple; he is different in that in addition to being a university don he was intimately connected with the Labour movement all his life, not only with its educational side in the Workers' Educational Association (like Temple), but also in the political and industrial side, and was at times involved in policy formation.[34] No one quite like him exists in the Labour movement now, but his spirit lives on, and in the controversies within it since the General Election of 1979 there are often appeals to recover the essence of what he stood for. The tutor of Ruskin College, Oxford, produced in 1982 a pamphlet from which I quote as an alternative to quoting myself. Tawney believed 'that economics raised issues of fundamental principle which could only be resolved by moral choice. History was a moral drama too, in which rival systems of belief contended for supremacy and irreconcilable interests clashed. In his (writings) . . . we are offered, in essence, a secular version of the Fall, a reverse utopianism in which commercial forces accomplish the destruction of communal solidarities, and society as a spiritual organism gives way to the notion of society as an economic machine'.[35] Although standing for a fundamental change in the philosophy of society, which in turn would lead to a new structure of economic organization, and always being unwilling to conceal or evade this for temporal electoral advantage, Tawney was a moderate in Labour political terms; his fear lest it be corrupted was a fear of its moral corruption rather than fear of semi-Marxist theorists who wanted to bind it to a programme derived from an over simplified economic and political analysis.

3. A critique of the Christian Socialist Movement

What does the 'mainstream' Christian Socialist Movement stand for these days? At the 1960 union it was (1) the common ownership of the major resources of the world (and there has been some discussion of the different forms this might take);[36] (2) a classless and just society; (3) human and racial equality; (4) the unity of Christian people (a new note); (5) friendship between east and west (this reflects the 'soft' line towards the

USSR); (6) abolition of nuclear weapons (a post 1945 element); (7) disarmament and world peace. Much of this is as general as being against sin and in favour of fellowship. Discussions of common ownership have, however, gone into some detail. Here the Scott Bader Commonwealth, founded in 1963, has had a lot of influence. It is a Northamptonshire firm in the specialist chemical industry, employing about four hundred and thirty. There is a maximum wage differential of seven to one, 60% of the profits are ploughed back into the business, and as much as is distributed in bonuses to employees is given to charities. More recently the Mondragon Co-operative in the Basque region of Spain has attracted notice. An Industrial Common Ownership Movement began in 1971; in 1976 an Act of Parliament facilitated it, and in 1978 a Co-operative Development agency was created. But it remains small.

COSPEC in 1980 stressed five points. (1) Equality of opportunity (this by itself could lead to a meritocracy, which would make for an unpleasant society); (2) workers' ownership (this raises the problem inherent in producers' co-operatives); (3) community control of wealth (here the problem of centralized power has to be dealt with); (4) a planned socialist economy (it has to be shown how the allocation of scarce resources is to be settled); (5) full participation in decision making (this is an important matter which bristles with difficulties, especially in a society subject to increasingly rapid social and technological change).[37]

There is a vacuum of both faith and policies in the Labour movement today. The reformist elements – Christian and secular – lost impetus after the creation of the outlines of a Welfare State after 1945. Now there is the defensive task of defending it against a right wing backlash. But merely to advocate a return seems unsatisfactory, and there is doubt both about ways of developing it and the nature of the economy needed to sustain it. The working class is not uniform. A generation of relative affluence has increased the gap between the haves and the have-nots in it, especially between those in work and those unemployed. Trade unions and professional associations are very conservative in their attitudes, and on the radical side the 'idols' of the USSR and more recently China have fallen and nothing has replaced them. Short-sighted economic nationalism is growing. Electorates do not want to be disturbed in their relatively recent affluence and demand incompatible things, and since no government can provide them they tend to react against the one in power. It is doubtful whether governments are given enough manoeuvering room, or enough time between elections, to handle the economy effectively. A question is raised as to whether our advanced industrial economies are becoming ungovernable. A further complication is caused by the powerful and often frenetic international commercial and financial forces which can shake even the largest economy. What in this situation is the legacy of the Christian Socialist Movement?

First of all it should be honoured for its boldness as a pioneer in grappling with the qualitatively new society which industrialism and urbanization created, and in most cases bringing theology to bear upon it. Sometimes a debate arises as to how far intellectual developments genuinely arise out of the discipline in question and how far they arise from external factors. I do not think this is a very profitable polarization. There are many conditioning factors in thought, and the development of psychology and of the social sciences had made us more aware of them. We can never be completely aware; for instance we can now see that amidst their many acute internal disagreements the Victorians held many pre-suppositions in common of which they were imperfectly aware. They were subject to culturally conditioning factors, of which the economic were the most pervasive. But conditioning factors are not determining factors. Just as we are firmly convinced that to some extent each of us can be an originator of his own decisions, so we can assume that theology has some independent influence on the thinking of those who take it seriously. It was a true theological insight of Maurice to condemn the erection of competitive laissez-faire into a law of God and a philosophy of individualism. But the Victorian era was on the whole a confident one, and the Christian socialists tended to share in the widespread belief in the perfectibility of man and thus not to counterbalance the utopian strain in socialist thought. That left conservatism to claim that it was the 'realistic' party, understanding the concept of original sin. Yet a moment's thought will reveal that it tells equally against the hierarchical and paternalistic elements in conservatism, and indicates the necessity of checks on the abuses of power, since no one is good enough to exercise authority over others unchecked. This is particularly apposite in the era of multinational companies. The Christian socialists were often 'soft' utopians in terms of building the kingdom of God, and more recently those who owed nothing to Maurice have been 'hard' utopians in accepting too simply the Marxist claim to be a 'scientific' analysis of the development of society.

It is the utopian element which has been one of the main reasons for Christian socialist groups to be as fissiparous as left wing groups in general, splitting over disputes as to the purest form of socialism. It is the recovery of the eschatological note in the understanding of the kingdom of God in the ministry of Jesus which has undermined the Christian basis for the utopianism. Unfortunately those Christians most actively involved in the Labour movement tended to be the least theologically minded and the most prey to secular assumptions. Politically Christian socialist groups have been too theoretical, too suspicious of political processes. Nor did their theory always come to grips with difficult issues. They did not see that conflicts of interest are inherent in any society, including socialist ones, and that it is necessary to create structures which can handle them creatively and which will harness individual and group self-interest in the cause of social justice.[38] Conflicts of interest between consumers and producers and between managers and managed are endemic. Also there are problems of government control over nationalized industries which were not appreciated in the talk of common ownership.[39] The other source of fissiparousness has been sectarianism. Christian socialist groups have been slow to learn from the ecumenical movement. And they have had other limitations. Sociologically they have been too clerical, too middle class and in practice too paternalistic.

It is perhaps in the economic field that the Christian socialists have been weakest. It is not just the tendency to run after popular, ephemeral and erroneous nostrums like Henry George's single tax or Major Douglas' social credit or – less fanciful – guild socialism, but the inability to grasp the distinction between competition and the free market erected into an overall philosophy, and the market in a properly controlled political and social environment as one of mankind's most useful devices for deciding a basic problem in any society, the allocation of relatively scarce resources between alternative uses. Talking of production for use and not for profit, which frequently recurs in Christian socialist writing, obscures this. The assumption that there is something necessarily sinister in profits, moreover, obscures the distinction between profit as a directive and profit as an incentive, and the role of an entrepreneur in the economic order.[40]

Nevertheless, in spite of these defects the fundamental point remains. In the Christian view the economic order is made for persons and by its effect on persons it must be judged. If its philosophy requires the treatment of labour (persons) as one factor of production exactly like land and capital (things) it must be condemned. Moreover in the Christian view what each person has in common under God is much more significant than any empirical differences between them; the expression of this in the social order tends towards a communal and egalitarian outlook, for the sake of social fellowship. The visions of most of the Christian socialists were on the right lines; much more practical wisdom is needed to translate them into social, political and economic policies.[41]

2

Christianity and Economic Man

I came to the conclusion in the first chapter that there are three main weaknesses in the legacy of Christian socialist thought. First, it shared too much of a pervasive Victorian optimism in the perfectibility of man. Marxism also shares this. The utopianism of the Christian socialists was a voluntaristic or 'soft' one, whereas those who were influenced by Marxism with its deterministic strains, and they were not many in this country, shared in its 'hard' utopianism. I shall say more on this theme in the last chapter. The next defect has been the ecclesiastical sectarian and clerical character of much of it, and this applies, as we shall see, to much social theology. Thirdly, there has been its weakness in grappling with fundamental economic problems which all societies have to solve, even though it was right to repudiate the overall philosophy of competitive individualism which was dominant in Victorian Britain. It is to the question of these basic economic problems that I now turn.

It is an important time to consider them. The failure of much socialist thought to do so, a weakness shared by so much of the Christian Socialist Movement, has been revealed by the disappointing economic history of the various centralized command economies which have been established since the Russian revolution of 1917. This, coupled with the fact that no developed capitalist country has moved beyond a welfare economy, means that we have no working model of what a democratic socialist economy looks like. Related to this lack is a revival of interest in the free market in the last decade, not merely as a useful technique but once again as the basis of an ideology. This is true of Britain but still more of the USA. Anyone trained in

33

economics is likely to see some merits in the free market, and I am no exception, but there is a vast difference between regarding it as a useful device in its place for dealing with part of a perennial economic problem which any society has to solve, and creating an entire philosophy of life on the basis of it. It is therefore of considerable importance not only to bring out weaknesses from not taking basic economic issues seriously, but also to warn against taking them too seriously by erecting far-reaching value judgments on an economic basis which it cannot bear. What is the role of economics? What can it do and what can it not do?

1. *The role of economics*

The basic economic problem of any society is the allocation of scarce resources, that is to say resources which are relatively scarce compared with the many possible uses of them. Which goods and services are to be produced? How to measure and match the demand for them with the supply of them? How to distribute the rewards of producing them? How to allocate resources between present and future consumption, that is to say between current and capital goods? On what basis can we cost them?

There is no problem about free goods, like air. The only air we pay for is in countries wealthy enough to afford air conditioning. And if the process of nuclear fusion, as distinct from the present one of nuclear fission, should prove practicable it would make energy so abundant as to begin to approximate to a free good. The technology to achieve this can be adumbrated but does not yet exist, and we do not at present know whether it is technically feasible, but the possibility of it is one of the most intriguing questions facing the next century. It is *relative* scarcity which constitutes the problem for the economist. To him the true cost of any particular good or service is all the other possible ones which have had to be foregone in order that these could be produced. The phrase 'opportunity costs' is often used of this concept.

The development of economic life can be traced from a primitive system of barter all the way to the development of a free market, with money as a means of exchange and a standard of value, in which ideally the play of consumer's demands and producer's supplies exactly match, by a process of buying and selling goods and services at a price which exactly matches what purchasers are willing to pay and suppliers willing to sell. The emphasis is on the unit at the margin; one more or one less would upset the potential equilibrium between demand and supply. So the price which clears the marginal unit is the crucial one. One classical economist built up his entire exposition of the subject from the example of a housewife going out to the market to buy a pound of fish.[1]

Theoretically the problem of maximizing scarce resources with alternative uses can be applied to almost every aspect of life, for instance the division of my time between prayer and action. Not long ago there was an intriguing book by an American economist who applied his techniques, among other issues, to the question of the decision to marry in relation to the expected benefits compared with the opportunities foregone by doing so,[2] but in general economists confine themselves to decisions which are subject to market considerations.

Economics considers itself as the science which deals with this basic problem of choice in the allocation of relatively scarce resources. As a science it wishes to be 'objective' and 'value free'. It does not wish to be concerned with ethical questions. It has nothing to say about *which* choices are made in the allocation of resources; as a science it takes as given whatever economic choices are made by human beings in the economic order. However two qualifications do have to be made at this point. One is relatively minor. The pure theory of economics in this pursuit of objectivity has become more and more mathematical, and in doing so has tended to take over from mathematics an aesthetic criterion of elegance in devising economic models. Much more important is the realization that there is in fact one implicit value in economic theory. It is efficiency; that is to say the avoidance of waste in using the relatively scarce resources which have alternative uses or, to put it another way, the maximization of one's resource potential. It seems a pity to the economist to adopt policies which end in paying more for goods and services than the equilibrium of the market would indicate, so that communities become poorer than they need be in terms of output secured at a given money

35

cost. But the economist always has to admit that efficiency is not the *only* value, and that people may well wish to put other values ahead of it. They may well, for instance, think that the undiluted pursuit of efficiency could lead to results which affront our sense of humanity. Purely as an economist he cannot settle priorities of value. But he is alert to the propensity of individuals and groups to disguise from themselves the economic costs of the policies they pursue, and their wish to both 'have their cake and eat it'. I myself would like to see in the prices of articles which are subsidized to the consumer an indication on the price tag of how much it is; or in the case of those where the producers have been subsidized, how much of the price is due to that; or where the government has raised the price by imposing levies on a nationalized industry as an alternative to raising taxes directly, how much is added to the price. To take three examples, how many of us know how much agriculture is subsidized, or the extra cost of keeping uneconomic coal mines open, or how much our gas prices are due to government financial policy? Only in the case of petrol does there seem to be much public awareness. I say this not necessarily to criticize any of these policies, but only with a desire that an electorate should be more aware of the economic costs of what is going on.

The price of the value-free position in economics, and the fondness for mathematical models which goes with it, is abstraction. There is an enormous gap between the assumptions of pure theory and what actually goes on in the world. If it is thought that to ape mathematics is the way to intellectual respectability a considerable price has to be paid. Perhaps we should pause to note that there has been a lot in our culture which has regarded anything connected with values to be so involved in a sea of relativity and subjectivism as to be not subject to serious intellectual enquiry, and has thought that methods of study appropriate to the natural sciences are alone capable of giving anything approaching assured knowledge. It is this situation which has led to prolonged discussions on the status and methods of the social sciences. Of these economics is the most developed, and it has gone furthest in seeking value-free scientific objectivity. Today this philosophy of the natural sciences is itself under vigorous scrutiny, though that is not our concern in this book. Our concern is with the relation of an economics which is value-free (apart from efficiency) to the actual working of the economic order, and its tendency to generate theories by generalization from abstract assumptions which are a long way from being capable of refutation in the sense required by Karl Popper.[3] The mathematical and computational work of econometrics has not produced impressive results. Intense arguments over refinements of economic models go on because of the problem of relating them to what is actually happening. For one thing there is a tendency to assume that things will continue as in the past, whereas the economy develops historically; things change, uncertainty is unavoidable, and what individuals expect about inevitable uncertainties affects things, and these expectations are themselves not certain. This is a main reason for differences of opinion on practical policy among economists, and for the old joke that if you get three economists together you will get four opinions, two of them from Keynes; or for President Truman's alleged remark that he needed a one-armed economist, not one who said 'on the one hand – and on the other hand'. If the economist is searching for stable relationships which can be used as a basis for prediction he faces the problem that his hypotheses can never be tested under laboratory conditions. Variables cannot be isolated and studied against an assumed stable background. Everything is on the move. Moreover the economist is part of what he is studying. As someone has said, his task is like that of a hen trying to lay an egg on an escalator.

These abstractions, however, are not pointless. It is useful to consider both the free market 'demand' economy and its opposite, the socialist 'command' economy as 'ideal types' (to use terminology borrowed from the sociologist Max Weber),[4] which can never be totally implemented. Consider the free market economy. First of all it pre-supposes a legal structure of law and order and property rights. This is generally realized. But it also pre-supposes a commitment to basic moral virtues, which is not so generally realized. There will be more to say about these. Beyond these, pure laissez-faire ideally involves among other things freely contracting individuals (what of families?), who have complete knowledge of the market, are able to move freely if necessary from place to place, and are completely rational in their attitudes to present wants as against future growth. I mention these implications not to discredit the whole idea of a market economy but to bring out the artificiality of ignoring these considerations and erecting an entire philosophy of life on what may turn out to be a useful human device for certain practical purposes.

The problem for the economist is to retain the intellectual standards of the ideal world of an abstract theoretical system whilst using his intellectual tools, with all their limits and their need of supplementation from other disciplines, to make as much sense as possible of the real world. In practice this is what he tries to do, but it is important for him and for the rest of us to understand the limits of his competence. J. M. Keynes has a much quoted remark to the effect that 'the ideas of economists and political philosophers, both when they are right and when they are wrong, are more powerful than is commonly understood . . . Practical men, who believe themselves to be quite exempt from any intellectual influences, are usually the slaves of some defunct economist.'[5]

There are three contributions the economist can make to human wisdom. He can bring out the basic problems of production, distribution, saving and investment which any society has to solve. One of the problems of Marxist states has been that there is little or nothing in Marxist economics on how to run a socialist economy, because Marx thought that such a society, moving into a communist one, would only be possible after capitalism had fulfilled its historic role of so vastly increasing human economic productivity that the problem of production would be solved. Because of this abundance there would be no opportunity costs and no division of labour. Competing interests would have disappeared and men would need no economic incentives or discipline. Marx says '. . . in communist society, where nobody has one exclusive sphere of activity but each can be accomplished in any branch he wishes, society regulates the general production and thus makes it possible for me to do one thing today and another tomorrow, to hunt in the morning, fish in the afternoon, rear cattle in the evening, criticize after dinner, just as I have a mind, without ever becoming hunter, fisherman, cowherd or critic'.[6]

As soon as Marxist states have established their revolutionary change and have had to tackle the routine problems of economic management and planning, they have run into difficulties for lack of analytical tools. Revolutionary zeal, as in Cuba or in the Great Leap Forward in China, is then of only limited use. Older forms of social organization, such as the customary obligations and reciprocal sharing of an African village, do not work with large economies, let alone those which are post-industrial revolution. Indeed one of the strengths of the market as a mechanism turns out to be the disadvantages of the alternatives to it.

The economist can also explore the implications of the choices that are in fact being made or proposed between relatively scarce resources, and expose incompatibilities in them. For instance it is clear that many electorates in advanced industrial economies want three things; a stable price level without inflation, full employment (apart from people changing jobs), and free collective bargaining. The three are incompatible. No government can provide them. Disgruntled electorates tend to throw out the one in power for not doing so. Any possible policy involves a choice between some mixture of the three. It is by pointing out the secondary consequences of the various choices available that the economist makes his contribution.

His third contribution is to expose economic nonsense when it appears. For a time, especially in the last major depression following the Wall Street crash of 1929, an economic theory propounded by an engineer, Major C. H. Douglas, called social credit, became popular although it could be refuted by any first-year student of economics. Yet a number of Christian thinkers adopted it uncritically. Another example is the report *The Limits to Growth*, published in 1972 by a private group called The Club of Rome, almost entirely technologists, which purported to forecast, on the basis of various extrapolations from contemporary trends, a crisis of industrial society within a hundred years because of the exhaustion of irreplaceable natural resources. It had serious economic flaws which have been thoroughly analysed, but it had a great effect for a short time in the Western world, particularly among the readers of the quality newspapers. Some of the ideas of the ecology movement, such as 'Friends of the Earth' have been unduly influenced by it, but not all. There are issues here which do need facing,[7] but not on the apocalyptic canvas of that first Club of Rome report.

In practice the economist is a tough-minded person with a sceptical turn of mind. He is alert to vested interests dressed up in high sounding policies. He is often a good chairman of commissions of enquiry for this reason. Of course he has to go further as a citizen in committing himself to specific value judgments and detailed choices. In his tough-minded impatience with the equivocations and rationalizations of individuals and groups in politics he is often liable to forget the limitations within which politicians move; that they have only limited instruments with which to operate and have to work within many political restraints, of which we shall have to say more. Sometimes, indeed, economists betray in their enthusiasm for the free market an extraordinary political naivete on the nature of power in political life. This, together with the limitations of their competence, purely as economists, in connection with economic and political policies, is an indication that they, like other experts, are not suitable by sole reason of their expertise to decide policy. We cannot do without their expertise, but we cannot put ourselves in their hands. Government by experts cannot work on the basis of their expertise alone. Judgment on the details of policy involves a mixture of value judgments brought alongside evaluations of the current situation, in the course of which the varying opinions of experts have to be assessed. In Western democratic societies this is left to the electorate.[8]

2. *The origin and development of the market economy*

It is worth spending a little time in contrasting this picture of the nature and significance of economics with the mediaeval background out of which it developed, and which was the inspiration of Christian social theology until the end of the seventeenth century. Mediaeval thought was never as unified as it is sometimes supposed, but certainly there was a far closer relation between Christian theology, the Christian church and social institutions than anything we know today, or could conceive of. There is a reality about the 'mediaeval synthesis', in which theology was the 'queen of the sciences' and laid down the broad parameters within which the other disciplines worked. In one sense it was not narrowly restrictive. Central to it in economic and political terms was a concern for justice, which was considered 'natural' to men and women, and which was woven into a *super* natural understanding of faith, hope and love, in a subtle blend of Christian thought with that of the classical world of Greece and Rome. So there was an elaboration of the theory of the just wage and the just price, (and of course of the just war).[9] But because the economy was changing so slowly as to be thought of as fixed and static, there was a tendency to assume that the *status quo* was just; so the aim of economic doctrines was to secure everyone in his station in life. It was the growth of merchant capitalism in the Italian city states, notably Venice, with its trade with the East, which began the break-up of this economic order. As the name capitalism indicates, it was the accumulation and use of capital for a long term investment which it was expected in the end would bring a vast return, as against current consumption, which produced the crunch economic issue, the question of the price to be charged for the use of money over time. That is to say the question of interest, or usury. The schoolmen had vetoed usury. This prohibition was not based so much on the Old Testament (which forbad the taking of interest only from fellow Israelites), nor on the New Testament (which assumes it, incidentally),[10] but on Aristotle who had said that money is barren, that breeding is unnatural for it, and therefore it is wrong to make a charge for the use of it. Note that the objection was not to tithes or ground rents (which were the equivalent of a productive loan), but to pure interest and to a certain return on the capital lent. Debenture stocks would be the epitome of what was condemned. Debates went on for a long time, and by the seventeenth century Christian thinking came round to admitting that in buying the just price was the market price. But it would not admit this in selling. So it never allowed the relevance of what a would-be profit-earning borrower was willing to pay for the use of money over time to the price (or interest) to be charged for it, but only the position of the lender. He was allowed to make certain charges in certain cases, but only with reference to his position, not that of the borrower.[11] Such teaching became increasingly irrelevant, in spite of the weight of church authority. The church herself was deeply in debt to usurers, who were usually Jewish because of the Christian prohibition of usury. Indeed it was the indebtedness of the church which sparked off the Reformation. Tetzel's Indulgence campaign was in aid of the Archbishop of Mainz's dues to the Papacy, which was itself heavily in debt to the Fugger family; and Tetzel's campaign was the occasion of Luther's protest with his ninety-five theses of 1517.

Calvin, on the other hand, regarded interest as a commercial necessity, and allowed it at a modest rate and with strict church-state supervision. Papal condemnations, however, continued, the last being in 1745 and 1838, though less and less notice was taken of them. It was only in 1891 in the Encyclical *Rerum Novarum* of Leo XIII that a new start was made in Papal social ethics. The Church of England took the strict mediaeval line until the Civil War, but the prohibition was unenforceable. If one wished to borrow money one had to pay interest. Gradually the term usury became confined to the charging of *excessive* interest. It was on this whole sorry tale of Christian irrelevance that R. H. Tawney in his Scott Holland lectures pronounced the verdict that 'the social teaching of the church had ceased to count because the church itself had ceased to think'.[12] Her economic teaching at the end of the seventeenth century was essentially similar to what it was at the end of the thirteenth century, frozen and lifeless.

It was against this background that the economic theory of mercantilism was developed in Protestant countries, which were experiencing the dynamics of merchant capitalism. This beggar-my-neighbour theory of economic life is still with us. Presupposing a fixed amount of trade, each country engaged in trying to gain a favourable balance of trade against others in trade wars of all against all, and to build up stocks of bullion. It is far from dead. Much of the trade practices of wealthy nations with respect to each other and to the Third World reflect a crude mercantilism, as do policies advocated by both right and left wing political parties.

However I pass on at once to Adam Smith as the founder of modern economics. It was he who elaborated the theory of the free market as the least bad way of running the economy. Because of the venality and short sightedness of individuals and of governments he favoured the settling of the basic economic issues as far as possible by the free market. He was helped in this by a deist framework of thought according to which if each pursued his own advantage, through the automatic device of the free market, an 'invisible hand' would ensure that the result was the promotion of the common good. 'It is not from the benevolence of the butcher and the baker that we expect our dinner, but from their regard for their own interests. We address ourselves not to their humanity but to their self-love, and never talk to them of our own necessities but of their advantages. Nobody but a beggar chooses to depend chiefly upon the benevolence of his fellow citizens.'[13] From this it was an easy step to see competition as the key to human economic life and as a law of God; and so we arrive at the ideology of laissez-faire, which is what F. D. Maurice criticized. At the time it was seen by Adam Smith and by others as a blow against arbitrary privileges enjoyed by an effete aristocracy; and the bourgeoisie in adopting it universalized their position, and thought they were liberating everyone from the shackles of the rigid economic order of the past. And that indeed is how it was to seem to many Christians in the nineteenth century, even though the ideology of economic man it propagated is of one who will only co-operate with others in so far as his self-interest requires. The government provides the framework of the law, order and defence, and a guaranteed system of property rights. Beyond this the appeal is to a philosophy of possessive individualism.[14] It is important to separate this from the conception of the market as a useful mechanism for solving some economic problems if it is set within a different value commitment and a much more extensive structural framework.

From the time of Adam Smith for rather more than a century the development of economics was linked with utilitarian political philosophy. Efforts were made to measure utility in terms of pleasure and satisfaction. Remember that marginal utility plays a great part in the theory of market equilibrium. But this ran into all the difficulties of classical utilitarianism in measuring pleasure, epitomized in the question J. S. Mill tried to solve, Is pushpin as good as poetry? Is it better to be a pig satisfied or a Socrates dissatisfied? It was largely due to the efforts of the Austrian school around the turn of the century that economic

43

theory was liberated from this association and the neutral position of a value free 'scientific' study was established.

This created a difficulty for welfare economics, whose existence I have not so far mentioned. Adam Smith's system of 'natural liberty' pre-supposed a divine hand, Providence; and Providence in the Christian tradition (including the deist version of it) is concerned with human welfare. In Bentham this notion had become secularized. He differentiated between a natural harmony of interests which would be achieved when people understood their economic interests correctly and acted appropriately, and an artificial harmony of interests which would have to be achieved by public sanctions when they didn't. Many years later a welfare economist like A. C. Pigou,[15] writing in terms of utility, came to the position that it was impossibly complex to take account of each person's utility preferences, but that since it is assumed that utility diminishes as one moves nearer and nearer the marginal unit, it is a fair assumption that one could increase the total amount of utility or happiness in the community by re-distributing income from the richer to the poorer. Therefore the problem was to achieve the right balance in doing this, since one would not wish to undermine the economic incentives on which the original theory of the market was based. However the next stage in the development of economic theory denied the possibility of making inter-personal comparisons of utility. As we have seen, it accepted whatever preferences were expressed in the higgling of the market, but had no comment on the values as such which were thereby expressed. This undermined the basis of welfare economics. An attempt has been made in political philosophy to revive a seventeenth-century social contract theory to establish what would be the supposed interests of individuals, prescinding from a society not yet formed. From this it is possible to argue a case on what is called the Pareto principle (after an early twentieth-century Italian economist), which would be not to make any alteration in the present economic set-up unless at least one person would gain, and no one lose by doing so. This is a highly conservative position and in effect rules out any major change. It is only plausible within the individualistic social and ethical pre-suppositions of society. Economics cannot solve questions of welfare. They involve wider political, philosophical and (a Christian would say) theological considerations.

These considerations are vital. It is clear that value free economics and value free markets pre-suppose not only a legal structure but a network of human communal values and obligations, which in this country were inherited from the Christian past.[16] This has not been realized and therefore the fact that the economic institutions do not foster them has not been thought about. Indeed the thoughtless preaching of competitive individualism undermines them. One of the best examples of the virtues needed to make the capitalist free enterprise system work is that of the Quakers who, in relation to their numbers, have made a very large contribution to the commercial and industrial development of the country. They were men and women of exceptional personal integrity, whose word was their bond, and who had a strong sense of public responsibility. These virtues were never as much in evidence as was desirable, and they seem less so today. The rapid social and technological changes of our time, the weakening of institutional religion, and the moral pluralism, to name three of the factors much studied by sociologists (especially sociologists of religion in their analyses of the process of secularization) has led the question to be asked, Where today is the source of disinterested goodwill to be found? One recent and cogent study by an economist thought there could be three: social ties, religious teaching, and a sense of civic duty. But he pointed out that modern mobile society tends to weaken social ties; he himself thought religion now too weak to contribute much; and he was left with a revived sense of civic duty, which is rather a frail hope.[17] Another sociologist, who is a specialist in the study of religious sects, thought at one time that they, as distinct from the mainstream churches, would be a source of the desired goodwill. However he has now become pessimistic about the sects as well, and in consequence pessimistic about the social future.[18]

3. Fundamental economic problems of market and command economies

The opposite of the ideal free market demand economy is the ideal centrally planned command one. Before considering that let us consider some of the problems the demand economy gives rise to and some it does not solve, after paying tribute to the efficiency of a market system in maximizing human productivity in using relatively scarce resources.

There are a number of collective demands with which it cannot deal. Defence is an obvious example. There are many more. It was health considerations which did most to undermine the pure theory of laissez-faire in the nineteenth century. It was impossible to deal with cholera on a liberal individualist basis, for it was no respecter of persons and was liable to spread from the poor to the rich. The demand economy also has great difficulty in dealing with what are called externalities, or the deleterious consequences of economic actions by one producer which affect others for the worse and which are not reflected (unless the market is deliberately interfered with by state policy) in the price level. Pollution is an obvious example. This is also no respecter of national boundaries. Prevailing wind currents bear our acid rain in the direction of Scandinavia and North Germany. The free market, moreover, has difficulties in seeing far enough ahead. Even if the future is discounted at the rate of about 10% per annum, it only means taking about fifteen years ahead into market considerations. Yet many projects need a longer perspective than that. Nuclear energy, and especially dealing with radio-active nuclear waste, is an obvious example. Difficult as it is to forecast more than a limited time ahead, most of us would think that we have a responsibility to future generations, at least as far as our grandchildren, to the extent that we can plausibly foresee the likely consequences of our actions.

Then, again, the free market system has not proceeded in a smooth way, but in a series of booms and slumps, which in the last century was almost a ten-year cycle. This means that, for example, in a slump men and women are threatened by unemployment and poverty in a way vital to their well-being through processes over which they have no control and circumstances which they could not avoid. Since 1918 we have not had a ten-year cycle, but a particularly vicious slump in 1929 and another one now. It is certainly arguable that government actions made the 1929 one worse and are making this one worse. But that does not mean that in principle there could not be better and less short-sighted government actions; nor that it can be right to subject people's lives to the vagaries of the trade cycle without remedial action. Indeed government actions are inevitable. If any country decided to adopt a totally free market policy it would come up against the fact that, whatever they say, every country subsidizes some of its industries and finds ways of protecting its home market. American actions, for instance, are different from President Reagan's theories.[19] The problem is how to minimize the perpetuation of the inefficient which these interferences usually entail.

Most people are aware of the inequalities of wealth and income which result from the free market system. Rights of inheritance tend to make this cumulative, and the system then works on the principle of 'to him that has shall be given', in a way of which the gospels were not thinking. Those who have wealth have a great pull on the market because they can bid for more luxuries than the poor can for necessities, as well as commanding the best attention in the basics of living – food, clothes, houses – and in personal services in education and medicine. Also the possession of capital tends to lead to the accumulation of more in a cumulative way, in spite of a number of stories of families which have gone from rags to riches and back to rags in three generations. Incomes have become more equal in this country, but we have not done much more with respect to the inequalities of wealth than re-distribute that of the top 1% among the top 5%.[20] How far this is considered a defect depends on a value judgment. My judgment is that men and women who are wise will think rather of their resemblances to their fellow human beings than of their differences from them, and this will give an egalitarian direction to their judgments about the direction of the distribution of goods and services. It is not, however, the only consideration. There is a lot to be said for another remark of J. M. Keynes. 'The political problem of mankind is to combine three things: economic efficiency, social justice, and individual liberty.'[21] If that is so, egalitarian tendencies still have their force and, I may add, are entirely consistent with the Judaeo-Christian affirmation that the most important thing about each person is that he or she is made in the image of God.

With wealth goes power; power to command economic resources, including those which influence opinions. This in turn relates to property rights. Without going into detail in the matter it is worth noting that the classical Christian defence of private property, that of St Thomas Aquinas,[22] pre-supposes the widest possible distribution of it, so that each person or family has so to speak a space round itself to express personal qualities. This is quite different from the distribution of wealth and property in Western industrial societies.[23]

These inadequacies of the free market are not the flaws alleged by the Christian socialist critique, which I think were mistaken. Christian socialists thought there was something unchristian in competition itself,[24] not distinguishing the falsity of thinking of it as the key to man's relation with man from the innocuous and indeed useful place it can have in human relationships. With their talk of production for use and not for profit they did not distinguish the usefulness of profit as a criterion for solving many problems of the allocation of economic resources from crude theories of private property. Lastly they talked about the motive of service to such an extent as not to consider the place of self-interest (and with it family interest) in human life. Christians read in the New Testament Jesus' summary of the Jewish Torah, 'You shall love your neighbour as yourself', yet have often found difficulty in thinking this through. There have been many discussions of the matter, but the essence of them is that without a proper self-affirmation it is not possible to relate adequately to others, or even to have a proper self to lose when it is necessary. Of course life is not all the time lived at the highest levels of either self-affirmation or self-sacrifice, and entire societies cannot operate economic and political structures which pre-suppose those levels of affirmation, though they should not exclude them. I have often quoted the sentence of William Temple, 'The art of government in fact is the art of so ordering life that self-interest prompts what justice demands.'[25] A good case can be made for maintaining that there is not a great deal of difference between the actions which would result from an enlightened pursuit of self-interest and those which would result from an other-regarding attitude.[26] But the exclusive pursuit of self-interest tends not to be enlightened; most self-interest is too crude and needs refining, and other-regarding motives, which tend to be weaker, need fostering. Moral and religious agencies in society have a major part to play here. Governments should devise institutions which help and do not hinder this process, and in particular find ways of harnessing self-interest to the most constructive uses. The free market is one such institution in its due place.

Advocates of this place often do their case a disservice by their political naiveté. They will not trust people as voters in economic matters, because they are so aware of the corruption of judgment by interests; they will trust them only as consumers. That is why they favour the automatic processes of the free market with its impersonal decisions. There are some reasons to support this position which will be mentioned in the next chapter, but they are far from decisive. It is clear that human beings when they are able to influence governments will not allow their vital interests to be settled by impersonal and automatic processes. Whatever their official ideologies, trade unions, professional associations functioning as trade unions, and management, all react in the same way. They want decisions which will have major economic consequences for them made in the *political* realm. That is why the verbal commitment to the more automatic processes of monetarism which we have seen in the last few years in Britain and the USA has been only imperfectly matched by deeds, and why a monetarist policy has been only partially followed.

The theory, however, is a strange return to the situation of 1929. Then monetarist policies were one element in intensifying the depression. After that we had a long period of Keynesian management of the economy which led to an unprecedented period of economic growth, until it began to be checked by the OPEC inspired oil price rise of 1973. The difficult political choices which this made necessary were fudged by Western governments, abetted by management and unions, so that we have seen a return to pre-Keynesian monetarism by the two administrations of Britain and the USA. We hear once more that because of the uncertainties of life it is best if governments do little, for if they have an active policy they will be sure to make a mess of it. There is even talk in the USA of a return to the Gold Standard in order to remove discretion over monetary matters from government hands. It does not need a Christian to point out that there was no golden age of the Gold Standard.[27] The pursuit of automatic economic decisions to this extent is the pursuit of a chimera. There is no escape from political decisions on economic problems. The free market itself is not a divine or 'natural' institution; it is a human device designed for particular human purposes and needing a well thought out

49

framework of political and economic institutions surrounding it.

On the other hand the command economies have run into difficulties. They operate detailed planning by rationing of materials and capital, and control of wages. The complexities of deciding everything by central planning are cumbersome in the extreme. There are said to be twelve million identifiably different products in the USSR needing between two and a half and three and a half million planned indicators at the centre. Hence the vast centralized bureaucracy. It is true that the development of computers has made the holding together of masses of simultaneously changing variables much easier, but it does nothing to solve the problem of innovation, which is a weak point of command economies because technical progress destabilizes the Plan. (By contrast demand economies are troubled by industrial espionage.) Also computers depend on the basic data which are fed into them, and if these have no rational basis there can be no rational outcome.

Moreover there are many other weak points. Because there is always a seller's market shortages (as distinct from relative scarcity) are endemic; quality is hard to achieve, except where there is a naturally homogeneous product like electricity, or where the central government is the direct customer as in armaments. Agriculture is handled badly because of the heterogeneous nature of the resources such as the varying quality of land and uncertain weather. There is a perpetual tendency to over-invest and neglect routine maintenance. Above all there is the problem of pricing. If prices are kept low because price rises are unpopular the result is that the privileged bureaucracy get the product, a black market and bribery develop, and a kind of barter system may spring up which even draconian police activity cannot suppress. No wonder that Nove says 'There is a long agenda awaiting socialist economists. They cannot even begin to face the real problems unless they openly reject the utopian elements of the Marxist tradition.'[28]

It is not only that Marx's picture of what amounts to an economic paradise where there are no economic problems because relative scarcity has been overcome, gives no guidance for running a socialist economy, but that his analysis of value in a capitalist society as distinct from the 'real' value of a product is faulty. His labour theory of value which is based upon the 'socially necessary labour time' involved in the production of a good or service has given rise to an immense debate, into which it is not possible to enter now. However the result has been that almost all discussions of economic issues in the socialist command economies have felt constrained to work within this framework, and have complicated the efforts to move away from the stifling centralized bureaucracy.[29] In practice the attempts to do so have had varied success. The Polish economy has been badly mishandled. An attempt was made to increase both investment and consumption at the same time, especially when Gierek succeeded Gomulko. The necessity of raising prices was not faced, and only heavy borrowing from the 'West' averted complete disaster. It does not appear that the various strains in Solidarity have faced this issue. Yugoslavia has experimented with a more decentralized system of Workers' Councils. It is hampered by the age-old rivalries of the six republics and two autonomous provinces which constitute the country, and where regionalism compounds the difficulty of arriving at rational economic decisions. The experiment is revealing some of the problems of workers' democracy. They are not the co-owners nor shareholders and their influence tends towards inflation and poor investment decisions because they want to keep things as they are; that is to say to keep their jobs if results are bad and to keep others from being added to the work force if they are good. They tend to show a lack of concern for the enterprise considered as a whole in relation to the economy as a whole and, indeed, it is not easy to see what either their real interests or the general interest is, as I have already mentioned. All complex economies face this problem.[30]

Hungary seems the most successful of the command economies. From 1968 there has been a New Economic Model which has confined central planning to key sectors, such as energy and transport. Almost alone among command economies Hungary has successfully achieved price rises to dampen excessive demand, and successfully handled the agricultural sector. There is no worker self-management. Recently one of Hungary's leading economists, Tibor Liska has advocated a form of entreprenurial socialism which would involve insecurity of *tenure*, though not of *income*, in every entrepreneurial or managerial job. Anyone would be free to bid to take over the resources if he thought he could do better with them, but he would have to guarantee his income to the previous entrepreneur, and pay the state the rent it charges for the use of them. Every citizen would have a basic personal inheritance; he could draw on this for entrepreneurial activity if he wished, or not. Obviously this system cannot apply to large units. It has already been implemented to a slight extent, but it remains to be seen how far the central authorities will tolerate it or will be fearful that it will undermine their power.[31]

From 1949–57 China followed the economic model of the USSR. Then came the Great Leap Forward from 1958, and relative economic chaos. The Cultural Revolution from 1966 was not much better. Now there seems to be an emphasis on agricultural production, and more attention to consumer goods, but whether there is any breakthrough in Chinese economics in dealing with the basic economic problems remains to be seen.[32] In all this there is little help from Marx as an economist. More is to be obtained from Marx as a sociologist, with his analysis of the alienation of the labourer in capitalist society, and the inhumanity of treating human beings as merely a factor of production in the sense in which land and capital are; because relationship is essentially a characteristic of human beings.

For the rest, in this very brief reflection, which is all that is possible, on the command economies there is the very important point to note, that the concentration of political and economic power in the same hands has sinister possibilities. It has proved extremely hard in these socialist command economies to arrive at checks on the abuse of power. So much is this the case that many socialists, having become disillusioned with centralized Marxist states, elaborate theories of a decentralized, minimal state verging on almost spontaneous local participatory decision making, which has no relation to the problems of advanced post-industrial societies.[33] There is talk of rule by 'the people', as if it is a unified group within which there are no conflicts of interest. Moreover the problem of harmonizing them in a roughly acceptable fashion is complicated by the sheer difficulty for different groups of knowing what their real interests are, because of the number and scale of inter-related factors.

However, the problems of running Western advanced economics are also severe. They have scarcely begun to cope with the problems of rapid technological change by devising social policies which prevent undue hardships on individuals and groups in adjusting to them. The result is defensive pressures on governments from right and left to cushion us against change. This means perpetuating inefficiency. The rigidities produced thereby are in the end a cause of unemployment. We are in fact not merely facing a cyclical depression which is bound to 'bottom out' before too long, but also a long-term structural change which is removing the routine physical and mental jobs on which half the working population have hitherto depended, and giving them to machines.[34] In the long run it is good that routine and tedious jobs are removed from persons and given to things, but in the short run it is producing the traumas of unemployment in almost all age groups. And it will be a long run unless with fair rapidity we move to a very different type of society, one which uses the personal qualities of the relatively unskilled and gives them a proper job which society is willing to pay for. Other policies, like a reduced working life, reduced hours of work, job sharing and the like are part of the answer, but by no means the whole of it. We are moving to a high productivity economy on a much narrower manufacturing base, in short into a service society. We cannot say to half the working population that they have nothing to contribute that we think worth paying for, so we will pay them a moderate amount to be idle. We could organize ourselves to organize their services, and we must, but we cannot do it on the basis of a philosophy of possessive individualism.

At present the newly affluent electorates of our Western societies are far from seeing this. Those in work cling to their relative affluence and yet are disgruntled, whether they are professional people or weekly wage earners. They like the social benefits but complain about the taxes necessary to service them. The root trouble is that, as Hirsch points out in the book I have mentioned, what he calls 'positional goods' which have been so much an incentive to economic effort, become less enjoyable the more they are shared. The more people opt to live in suburbia the more the urban sprawl grows; the more have cars the more the roads get choked by traffic blocks; the more descend on a beauty spot the more its beauty is threatened. In his phrase, 'if everyone stands on tip toe no one sees any better'. According to him the 'invisible hand' only worked in the early stages of the industrial revolution. I say that now we need a visible hand. It is not so much the social limits to growth that we are reaching as the social limits to private consumption. This is another way of pointing to the necessity of consciously developing a service society (the drift is that way in any case). It is entirely congenial to Christian ways of thinking, which hold that we should live in a community of giving and receiving, and not try to be as independent of everyone else as we can and not 'beholden' to others.

The market will remain a useful device, provided it is treated as a servant and not as a master. However I see no way of dealing with the problem of the economy without some wages and prices policy. If the price control mimics the market, as far as possible, it will mean that managers cannot automatically pass on costs but must set out to improve efficiency; and this is very like introducing profit criteria into a command economy. On the other hand 'free collective bargaining' is an appropriate concept in a free market economy (for individual bargaining in wages would be socially and politically absurd), but not for the types of mixed economy which we have been adumbrating. In a command economy it does not exist at all. The political difficulties of a wages and prices policy cannot be over estimated. Think of the difficulty of getting agreement on income relativities, and of changing them as conditions change. Scepticism is understandable, but the task must be attempted.[35]

Finally, the responsibilities of advanced industrial countries for the two-thirds rest of the world must at least be mentioned. 37% of Christians at present live in the poor 'south', and probably more than half will by the year 2000. Some Christians argue that no one should live more affluently than everyone in the world could conceivably live. Apart from the difficulty of working this out, it is not certain that reduced spending by the more affluent in itself helps the poor. The worst times in developing countries is when demand is slack in the rich ones. But the nature of the demand is vital. Lobbying for far-seeing policies on the part of the wealthy is important, more important than voluntary aid, though that is important too. The eight hundred millions of people who are absolutely poor, whose basic needs are unmet, is the most pressing issue facing us, apart from nuclear warfare.[36] They and we are living in what is increasingly one world.

Peasants listening to short wave radios in Bangladesh hear much the same world news as we see on our TV screens. It is true that there are limits to what the wealthy countries can do, and a lot must be done by the poorer ones themselves. Also resentment at our dominance and short sightedness may lead them into policies of self-reliance which will mean slower growth, so we need to take care. And their own domestic policies may be corrupt and unjust. But it would be possible by wise policies to break the 'sound barrier' of absolute poverty in the middle income countries, and in all but 15–20% of the population of the lesser developed countries, by the year 2000. Domestic and international politics connect. Part of the trouble with implementing the proposals of the Brandt Reports,[37] and the more radical ones advanced by some critics of them, is that although the result in the end would be to the benefit of all, particular sections of the affluent countries would suffer and, since we have no social policies to cushion the adjustment, they resist. So little is done. Yet there could hardly be a nobler task than removing abject poverty and the oppression that goes with it from the backs of the majority of those at present suffering under it.

However, what I have been saying in this chapter is far from an outlook which has grown quickly in the last four or five years, that of what I call the new radical right. It is to this that I turn next.

3

The New Radical Right

The discussion in the first chapter on the legacy of the Christian
Socialist Movement concluded that one of its weaknesses was an
inability to identify and reflect on the fundamental economic
problems which any society has to solve. That led in the course
of the second chapter to a discussion of the scope and limits of
economics as a discipline. I mentioned that it was both necessary
to take economics seriously and also to subject it to a theological
critique. I begin this third chapter by referring to another tradition of Christian social theology which flourished in the early
part of the nineteenth century and which did make the mistake
of taking the burgeoning discipline of economics too uncritically.
It also foreshadows in many ways the new radical right, which is
the main theme of this chapter.

1. Christian political economy

I have more than once referred to the absence of a Christian
social theology after the traditional one faded out at the end of
the seventeenth century, until a new beginning was made with
F. D. Maurice and the Christian socialists of 1948–54. By that I
meant a tradition which on a theological basis was prepared to
advance a critique of the current economic institutions of society
which had become the basis of an overall philosophy of life. We
need to note, however, that in the early nineteenth century there
did develop another social theology. It was oblivious of the
former and by then vanished traditional Christian social doctrine, and instead of erecting a critique of the new individualistic
pre-suppositions deriving from the new economics, it accepted

them, took the economics as a proven 'science', and tried to establish a theodicy on the basis of it. By taking the new economics too uncritically it thus made the opposite mistake to that of the Christian socialists, which was not to take it seriously enough.

Major contributions to the development of economics were actually made by clergymen most, but not all, of them of the Church of England. At this time it was possible for the clergy to do this. It required the disciplined thought of an able and well-educated mind on economic problems. There were no specialists. The more able clergy possessed these qualities and some of them turned their attention to the new economics which was superseding mercantilism.[1] That is why J. M. Keynes in a letter to William Temple could refer to the fact that many of his clerical predecessors had made a contribution to economics.[2] In addition many of them made it the basis of a social theology. T. R. Malthus is the figure who comes most prominently to mind. The first edition of his *Essay on Population* appeared in 1798.[3] His book was a defence of the *status quo* against the equality in the French Revolution's triad of liberty, equality and fraternity, and in particular against Godwin's doctrine of human perfectibility. Malthus held that a state of equal liberty and equal justice could not in principle be achieved or, if it were, it would quickly revert. Poverty and inequality are inevitable because population unchecked increases at a geometrical rate and subsistence only at an arithmetical rate. Population will always tend to increase to the limit of subsistence, so no permanent improvement is possible in the lot of the poor. Population growth is checked by necessary misery and probable vice. He went on to argue in his last two chapters that this situation is necessary under Providence for the full intellectual and spiritual development of the human race, but he withdrew these chapters in the later editions of the book, and it was left to others to take up the theodicy. Among these William Paley,[4] William Whewell,[5] J. B. Sumner,[6] Edward Copleston,[7] Richard Whateley,[8] and Thomas Chalmers,[9] were prominent. William Paley tended to argue from Nature (with a capital N) that these features of human life were necessary to make it a state of discipline and probation. J. B. Sumner as an evangelical argued it more on the basis of scripture. Part of his sub-title refers to the 'Consistency of the Principle of Population with the Wisdom and Goodness of the Deity'. Copleston and

Whateley, as enthusiastic as Malthus on the importance of private property and the appeal to self-interest, wrote of the folly of embodying benevolence in law, especially with respect to the Poor Laws. Chalmers, the Church of Scotland minister (who was later to lead the Disruption in 1843) stressed prudence and moral virtue, not legal provisions, as remedies for individual misfortunes. The poor have no legal rights to subsistence, otherwise compassion would be superfluous. His *Political Economy* appeared in 1832, and his *Bridgewater Treatises* in 1833. No significant additions were made to Christian political economy after that, though its ideas triumphed after its exponents had mostly died. There was a time lag. It was these ideas which were flourishing when, fifteen years later, the Christian Socialist Movement started. The proponents of Christian political economy assumed that Malthus, whose was the intellectual force behind them, was expounding a securely established science with which it was necessary for theologians to come to terms, even if they did not always like its implications.[10] But caution is necessary. Theologians either need the necessary competence themselves, or to acquire it through inter-disciplinary consultation, to keep abreast with what is happening in the sciences. If they do not possess it they may become irrelevant (as Tawney said) or, on the other hand, they will not have the wisdom to uncover hidden ideologies which often lurk undetected in the sciences, and particularly in the social sciences. Expertise must be listened to, but not uncritically.

Theologians have also suffered from a further handicap, a tendency to assume existing social arrangements to exhibit too unequivocally the divine intention. This is particularly unfortunate in a period of rapid social change which is characteristic of all industrial societies, and those other societies which they drag along in their wake; that is to say most societies. Theologians can thus be caught out by failing to perceive how things are changing. For example, in the USA Francis Wayland argued in 1837 that it is the divine intention that a large section of the human race should be employed in agriculture because it has the fewest temptations. In that case the British with less than 3% employed in it today are peculiarly chosen for divine temptation.[11]

The theology which lay behind the Christian political

economists was that poverty and social inequality are due to the Fall, but that they are also a divine contrivance for providing a discipline which will bring out the best in people. Hence the institutions of competition and private property are socially beneficial. At the same time true happiness does not depend on material possessions but on moral worth, especially that which is the fruit of the Protestant faith. The universality of the Christian faith indicated that these laws of God must be universally applicable. This outlook fitted in well with the developing philosophy or ideology of laissez-faire and helped clergy such as I have mentioned to develop it. Such an outlook had lost touch with traditional Christian social theology, whose erosion was examined by R. H. Tawney in the first Scott Holland lectures. I do not think anything is gained by maintaining either that theology can be decisive in influencing social and economic changes or that it is so conditioned by them as to be of negligible influence. Rather the point is that theology never operates as a 'pure' discipline but always in a social, economic and political context. Economic factors are very powerful and unless we are alert to them we shall succumb to them. In this instance the vigorous and raw forces of the new industrial civilization had eroded traditional Christian wisdom (which had lacked intellectual vigour to cope with the rapid social changes), and there were not sufficient transcendent resources left to call them in question. The Christian socialists were right to protest on this basic point.

2. *The denigration of politics by the radical right*

The last few years have seen an astonishing change in public opinion in this country in the area of economics and politics. The broad consensus which was called Butskellism, from the time when R. A. Butler and Hugh Gaitskell were leading figures in the Tory and Labour parties respectively, has almost disappeared. That consensus concerned the essence of a Welfare State,[12] and the necessity to achieve it by re-distribution of income by the state. It was expressed in phrases like 'fair shares', 'equal opportunities', 'meeting needs regardless of ability to pay'. Full employment was a commitment. It is now apparent that it was the steady economic growth for a quarter of a century from about 1948–1973 which enabled it to flourish. Then came the check in growth. It was due to the way the USA chose to finance the Vietnam war, and the way the Western powers together with the USA met the drastic oil price rise imposed by OPEC by carrying on as if no reduction in the standard of living through extra taxation was needed, and by increasing the supply of money in circulation instead. The result was inflation. The effort to deal with that has led to a resuscitation of theories of money management which flourished at the time of the 1929 economic collapse and were discredited then by making it worse. They have made the latest recession worse. It is a depressing picture.

There has also been a cultural backlash against the mood of the 1950s and 1960s. That mood was pragmatic, postivist, agnostic, plural (the more hostile term is 'permissive'), and to some extent meritocratic. It was disposed to stress the complexity and intractability of problems, even if the expectation of being able to live with them and make some progress in dealing with them was present. Now simple theories and moral absolutes are more in favour.

The USA has seen the same tendency, though it never approached a consensus like Butskellism. My comments will be confined to these two countries. A thorough comparative study of all the Western advanced industrial countries would be far too big an undertaking. One feature that is common to both countries is that a number of exponents of the new right were formerly of the old left.[13] They seemed when they were on the left to have had excessive expectations of what can be politically achieved in the economic field. When the going got tougher and it became apparent that these expectations were not going to be realized they came for the first time upon resuscitated arguments from the right which had been shown to be inadequate in the post-1929 depression, and took them up with no more discrimination than the opinions they had previously held.[14] The general terms of public discussion have clearly changed. It is depressing because I now find myself, shortly after retirement, presented with arguments which I used to hear as an undergraduate and which I mistakenly thought had been settled. Had I been giving the Scott Holland lectures ten years ago it would never have occurred to me to deal with 'the radical right'. But in 1983 it would seem unreal not to deal with it if one is discussing the broad issues of church and society in the late twentieth century with special reference to Christianity and the economic order.

A pre-supposition behind the thought of the radical right is that economic undertakings in private hands should be the norm, and what is in public hands is suspect. Governments are only competent over a narrow area. I have indeed heard it argued that the free market system is the only economic one which could operate without a state at all. This surprising alliance with the most wildly utopian of all leftish political theories, anarchism, had better be passed over quickly as too fanciful for serious study. Obviously opinions as to the proper limits of government activity in the economic field vary. It depends on how extensive are the range of issues that we consider the market unable to discharge. I mentioned some in the last chapter, including what are known as 'externalities' or 'neighbourhood effects', which would include things like noise and pollution. Again a realistic analysis of how things actually work might lead us to think that governments might have to act quite drastically in order to preserve the equilibria of the market as against various restrictive practices of both management and labour. The anti-Trust laws in the USA have at times been implemented vigorously. Again it is possible to be more radical and to argue that concentrations of wealth and power need to be broken up if the market is to operate effectively. Those who take this attitude would begin to come closer to those in the socialist command economies who want to move away from their rigidities and allow more play to market factors. Not many go so far as yet.

The suspicion of government enterprises and controls arises from the charge that they lack efficiency, are too subject to the pressure of vested interests, and lead to too much power insufficiently subject to check. Governments can fudge their mistakes. They are in no danger of going out of business as a result of them. Much of their activity is not easily subject to efficiency checks and this leads to over-manning. It is also much more dangerous to be disliked by your neighbour in a command economy, because he might well be able to get at you politically, whereas the market acts impersonally, oblivious of personal likes and dislikes. Moreover as consumers in the market the connection between one's decisions and their result is direct and immediate, whereas in politics it is remote. In politics we vote occasionally and for a whole package. Parties come into power with what they claim is a mandate from the electorate, with a variegated series of proposals which may take them four or five years to implement, and perhaps with well under half the electorate voting for them. In the market we are 'voting' constantly and precisely by the way we spend our money. Also because in politics the connection between the action of voting and its consequences is so much more distant, voting is much more irresponsible. It is a way of being moral on the cheap. In the market we have to pay for what we opt for. In politics we can vote for funds for this and that when the cost to ourselves is minimal. Indeed it is hard to be aware of the opportunity costs. The argument is pressed further. The more the role of the state is extended, the more we risk tearing apart the social fabric. Political parties with their eyes on opinion polls are tempted to offer prizes to everyone. Rival economic groups organize who cannot be appeased and whose demands are incompatible. We are in danger of being ungovernable. Political democracy becomes an unprincipled auction. To Hayek, whom I shall mention more fully in a moment, this is now a greater threat than the centralized planning he feared in his earlier book of a generation ago.[15]

There is a good deal to be said for all these points even though in the end they amount to an inordinate denigration of politics. The radical right contrasts the purity of the free market with the corruptions of politics. When, however, we ask how the market actually operates, we could produce just as vigorous a catalogue of log rolling, price fixing, oligopolies and monopolies, abuses of power and the like. The market economies in practice are very far from laissez-faire states. Britain and the USA in the nineteenth century were the nearest thing to laissez-faire states,[16] and there were special circumstances in each caes. Britain had an industrial lead through being the first with an industrial revolution, and the USA had the enormous expansive possibilities of the advancing frontier. The theory of laissez-faire atomizes the relation of person to person in a way which goes against the richest experiences of human life. It is no wonder that it is found insupportable. Management in practice repudiates it and labour has never accepted it. There is not the slightest chance of it being operated, and those who argue as if it were a serious option are wasting their time. A lot of self-deception goes on among those who use its language. The bluff needs to be called.

Faced with these criticisms of politics we have to ask, What is the alternative? Adam Smith, it will be recalled, advocated the free market as the least bad way of running the economy because of the venality of governments. Two hundred years have gone by since then. Now the argument has to go the other way. *Some* form of social welfare economy is the least bad way of running the economy. Whether it should be a social market economy (as the West Germans call it), or a democratic socialist one (of which I suppose Sweden has been the nearest to an example, but a far from complete one), is a further question. Nevertheless, in spite of the political problems it raises, to which we should address ourselves, people acting as voters, not just as consumers, must tame the pathological features of the market whilst allowing a proper place for it.

Political scepticism also has roots in a conservative philosophy which stresses an organic, not an individualistic, account of human relationships, and a reverence for established customs and institutions.[17] It is ironical that conservatives with these views should be part of a movement which advocates a free market, which has no respect for organic relationships and established institutions, but dissolves them into discrete individuals and their personal market preferences. A further element in a scepticism of the possibilities of political achievements is an emphasis, particularly by conservatives with a Christian outlook, on the radical moral imperfection of humankind, expressed in the misleading term 'original sin'.[18] However, a brief reflection on the doctrine leads to the conclusion that human beings should not be allowed to exercise power over others unchecked because no one is good enough to do this. Conservatives therefore need to pay as much attention to it as Liberals and Socialists do. It does not specially favour them.

3. *The economic virtues according to the radical right*

Turning from the negative denigration of politics by the radical right to its positive appreciation of the free market we need to recall and extend some of the theories mentioned in the last chapter. The stress is on efficiency and growth. This is a positive sum game. Everyone benefits. The free market is not so much an efficient device for allocating existing scarce resources, though it is that (even a computer could not do it as well); it is a technique for innovation, for discovery, for making ever more efficient use of resources. Its impersonality is its greatest blessing. Benevolence is weak and partial, whereas the market is universal and undifferentiating between persons. The unknown, the unattractive, the unimportant, the despised minority, will all have their wants served by it. The impersonality of the market is its advantage because our knowledge is so limited that we could not be consistent in taking personal factors into consideration.[19] Further, a protective attitude towards the poor savours of paternalism. The critic of the market finds the tables turned on him. If he says inequalities of income and wealth distort the market he is told that redistribution of income reduces investment and productivity and thus harms the poor by depriving them of opportunities. It is said that attempting to interfere with the market by, for instance, establishing a ceiling on profits only leads to inefficiency, and that will also hamper the poor. If speculation is criticized, the reply is that its effect is to dampen oscillations of price by acting as a kind of distant early warning system of likely market changes. If middlemen are reproached, we are told that by relocating things they change their value according to consumers' preferences.

Once again we have to say that in so far as these are advantages it is important not to lose sight of them, so long as we remember that the pure theory of the market is an 'ideal' system, prescinding from all questions of politics and power, and ignoring the corporate relationships of mankind.

Similarly the evils of inflation are real enough, though drawing attention to them is not the monopoly of the radical right. A small and steady rise in the price level (say 3% per annum) is no particular problem and may even be a stimulus to economic activity. Nor is a rise which is unexpected particularly disastrous. But when rises of much more than 5% per annum, or still more, 10%, 15%, or 20%, are expected, they are discounted and allowed for in advance in wages and prices, and the process feeds upon itself. The people who gain are then the lucky and the unscrupulous. Those who are unscrupulous are those who use their power to make maximum temporary gains. I say temporary because in the end others catch up with them, or threaten to, and no one is better off; except for the fact that those powerful enough to lead the way are pushing ahead again. The process is cumulative and radically de-stabilizing. Some professional groups are able to use power in this way, as are certain groups of workers. The medical profession and the miners have tended to set the pace. Printing workers and electric power engineers are another two powerful groups.

Luck also plays a considerable part in the theory of the market economy. One of the basic points made by its advocates is that economic rewards in the market cannot be related to merit. (And, of course, egalitarians have never wanted this anyway; in their view a meritocracy would be a most unpleasant society.) Milton Friedman stresses that market results have nothing to do with justice, but with skill and chance. Justice is concerned with the protection of property and the enforcement of contracts.[20] Hayek similarly says market rewards depend upon a mixture of effort, ability and luck. Justice and injustice can only result from deliberate action, whereas the market is impersonal. Welfare is therefore a matter of benevolence or charity, not justice. It is a gift, not a right.

Hayek realizes that the market is a human institution, like law and language, whereas some of its defenders write as if it were not a human invention but would be the 'natural' and spontaneous result of human behaviour if governments did not meddle with it. The assumption behind this is that human beings can be essentially analysed as separate and individual monads prior to any human contacts or social institutions.[21] It is this kind of thinking which has led to a new stress on the social contract theory which developed in the seventeenth century after the breakdown of mediaeval political philosophy and economy. Human beings are pictured as individuals in a state of nature voluntarily deciding on the basis of a rational agreement to set up a state, to avoid a war of all against all, and to safeguard the personal liberties and property of each individual. In order to do this it is necessary that each agrees to safeguarding that of others. John Rawls pictures individuals choosing, under a veil of ignorance of what their own position in society would be, a basis for that society which would maximize their ability to achieve their ends even if it turned out that they belonged to the less privileged strata. Liberty is his fundamental value. But for the rest he arrives at a fairly radical position, according to which inequalities could only be justified if they were to the benefit of the least advantaged. Concern for others does not enter into it, merely a rational calculation of the best basis for being sure of achieving as much as possible of one's own interests.[22]

There has been an immense discussion of Rawls. One issue has been whether he has established his principles within his own assumptions. I myself doubt whether he has. But for the Christian two things are disconcerting about Rawls. One is the social contract theory itself, until one realizes it is as much an aetiological myth as is the account of the Fall in Genesis. If Christians can go on using the doctrine of the Fall, as I assume they can, provided they know what they are doing, so presumably may political philosophers use the myth of the social contract. The trouble with it is that it is an inadequate myth in its basic individualistic assumptions about human beings. Men and women mature as persons because of the structures of human and social relationships through which they are formed before they have any personal knowledge of the fact; and their fullness as persons lies in all that their relationships enable them to become.[23] The other disconcerting feature is the absence of any call for altruism in Rawls' basic assumptions. Strong as self-concern is in human beings, beyond what is necessary and proper to them, the element of altruism is there too. But it is less strong and it needs developing. Christianity did not invent it. It deepens and strengthens the appeal to it. Any basic principles and structures of human life which do not draw on it are doing less than justice to our humanity. Indeed that is what is wrong with turning the institute of the free market into an entire philosophy of life; its sole appeal is to self-interest.

However if Christians are liable to be disconcerted with aspects of Rawls, they will be even more so by his extreme libertarian critic Robert Nozick,[24] not least because he bases his case on a respect for persons as ends in themselves, a phrase often on the lips of Christians. He argues that respect for persons as ends in themselves means respect for their inviolable rights (and they in turn must respect the inviolable rights of others, and a minimum state may be needed to enforce this). These rights include the right to one's own body and to the property which arises from one's own labour.[25] It follows that any compulsory re-distribution of property through the tax system is ruled out because my own property is being used for the benefit of others without my consent. There is no right to welfare. That must be left to private benevolence. I have the negative right not to be killed; but not to more than that. Positive welfare rights would mean that I have a right to the bodily labour of others. (This last point is one held by others than Nozick; that genuine rights must be negative ones, involving duties by others which are in principle always able to be fulfilled, since they amount to refraining from doing something. Positive duties might be incapable of being fulfilled.)

This is if possible an even more extreme individualist picture of a human being. There are certain forms of degenerate Protestantism which are deceived by it (especially in the USA), which have been corrupted by the philosophy of capitalism and which would have horrified Luther or Calvin, but leaving that aside for the moment we may note that a trio of political philosophers from Manchester University has produced a reasoned answer to Nozick.[26] They make the obvious point about the unreality of trying to isolate individual property rights through the labour involved in complex processes of production. They go on to argue that there are basic needs without which the individual cannot exercise basic rights; these include not only Nozick's physical survival but also the position to be able to choose values for oneself, and that means a certain space in which one can be autonomous. That in turn means that a certain level of food, shelter, health care and education is required before one can act like a Nozick man. And Plant arrives at the maxim: 'Each person has an equal basic right to the satisfaction of those needs which are necessary to the pursuit of any goods or values.' This does not imply an equal provision, and leaves many questions for further development, but it does provide the foundation for a minimum Welfare State in terms which are addressed to those attracted by Nozick's argument.

However there are other points to be made against these arguments of the radical right. Against Hayek, and all those who stress the hidden wisdom of established institutions, we can ask them why – unless they are totally reactionary and immobilist – they deny the possibility that welfare capitalism may not itself have developed some hidden wisdom in the course of a generation.

Is it not possible that the wisdom may indicate flaws which call for improving rather than dismantling it, as the new right wishes? Again, if one sets up a market to achieve certain purposes within a wider whole, why does its impersonality mean that we can have no conception of social justice, but must confine justice to the realm of order and the maintenance of contracts? Why cannot we set out corporately to deal with the 'bad luck' effects of the market? Why must this remain a matter of private benevolence? Thirdly, is there not something appropriate in the way modern society has moved back from the position where citizens are related by contract to a renewal of a relationship by status? It is true that the pre-industrial hierarchical relation of status was too confining and too immobile in its injustices. The movement from status to contract was a liberation in comparison. But the price was too high. It left most people too unprotected against the vicissitudes of life and the inequalities of power.[27] A welfare society which at least guarantees some minimum standard to a citizen as of right, below which he will not be allowed to fall, is an improvement. It is more important than maximum economic output from scarce resources.[28] Finally there is the argument I have just mentioned that the plurality of values in the modern world, which as far as possible needs respecting, does not obscure the fact that there are certain goods necessary for the pursuit of any values.

The new radical right goes on the offensive against those who criticize the present economic order on the grounds of social justice. Its own criticisms of it are on the grounds of liberty, and efficiency in maximizing production; it holds that justice, apart from basic legal justice, should be left to private benevolence. Those who criticize it on the grounds of justice are said to be a 'new class', a cultural elite made up of intellectuals, those connected with the communications media, and counselling folk; all people who are hostile to capitalism and business enterprise, despising entrepreneurial skills. Many are in public sector employment for whom more government spending means more jobs. They encourage idealistic expectations, and ignore problems which would be endemic in any social order. They have a vested interest in portraying social ills. They are envious of scientists and engineers who work for private enterprise and receive higher salaries than in the public sector. They do not have much political power, but hope to gain more by alliance with disaffected minorities. Sometimes it is alleged that Marxism is a useful weapon to them. This last comment is more likely to come from the USA, where people are more inclined to find reds under the bed and to equate social criticism with communism than is the case in Britain. And indeed the whole polemic against the new class is more characteristic of the USA, but it is heard here.[29]

The charge has some force against any intellectuals who assume that they are free of vested social and intellectual interests because they are neither workers for a wage, nor managers, nor capitalists. Such a belief is often found in academic circles, and it is the one weakness of that otherwise path-breaking book of 1936, Karl Mannheim's *Ideology and Utopia*, that in it at times he wrote as if the educated intelligentsia could be free from either ideologies or utopias.[30] No one, no group, no class can be purely rational, disembodied reasoners unaffected by any elements in its economic, social and cultural situation. But to be aware of this is to be able partially to overcome it, which is better than being unaware. Nor does the charge dispose of the social criticisms made by the new class. I would expect salaried workers with relatively modest pay and interesting and demanding jobs to be inclined to the left politically if they were at all sensitive to the disadvantaged situation of so many of their fellow citizens. That of itself neither supports nor disposes of their charges, nor does it necessarily endorse the remedies they suggest. All are subject to scrutiny. But to dismiss them as the product of envy and a desire for power is to trivialize serious issues, and savours of a desperate search for weapons by the radical right.

The new radical right seems to be largely a return to the seventeenth century. The theorists of it, however, do recognize what has by no means always been recognized, that the free market economy which it advocates pre-supposes moral values which it does not generate itself. I would say it is often oblivious of them, and in fact tends to undermine them.[31] Hayek says that there are two such moral values: the first is that of individual responsibility, and the second that the worth of individuals does *not* correspond to whatever material rewards they draw from the market economy. Clearly both of these are congenial to the Christian faith, which holds to the responsibility of the Christian to God for living his life and following his conscience. No one can live someone else's life for them. It also denies, at least in theory, that a person's status in society and before God is related to his income or wealth. In practice things work out differently in their social and usually in their religious expression, and it is perverse to abandon any attempt to relate a fundamental affirmation about the status of the person to the structures of economic life.

4. The spirituality of the radical right

There is also a far-reaching positive claim for the moral virtues of capitalism, far-removed from the mere realization that it presupposes some which need to come from elsewhere. It has become popular in the USA through the book *Wealth and Poverty* by George Gilder. He maintains that Adam Smith undersold capitalism in his emphasis on self-interest rather than altruistic creativity which is really its foundation. He also subordinated a higher and more complex level of activity – the creation of value – to a lower level, its measurement and distribution.[32] People who live in a free society can do so only if they believe it is a just society in which power, privilege and property are distributed by morally satisfactory criteria. Capitalism does in fact ensure this. It 'begins with giving. Not from greed, avarice or even self-love can one expect the rewards of commerce, but from a spirit closely akin to altruism'. . . . 'Not taking but giving, risking, and creating are the characteristic role of the capitalist . . .'[33] 'Capitalism begins with a gift and continues with competition in giving. These competitions succeed in generating new wealth largely to the extent that they are contests of *altruism* . . . A gift will only elicit a greater response if it is based on the needs of the recipient. The most successful gifts are when the giver fulfils an unknown, unexpressed or even unconscious need or desire of the recipient.'[34] The circle of giving (the profits of the economy) will grow as long as the gifts are consistently valued more by the receivers than the givers.[35] The giver must forego immediate gratification in order to produce goods of value to the beneficiaries. Capitalism depends upon supplying first and getting later. 'Capitalists are motivated not chiefly by the desire to consume wealth . . . but by the freedom and power to consummate their entrepreneurial ideas.'[36] The grasping or hoarding rich man is the antithesis of capitalism.[37] The investor cannot be fundamentally selfish or he will eschew initiatives and ventures in innovation and go for art, real estate and foreign retreats.[38]

Gilder is not against 'sensible' levels of welfare benefits. They relieve people of coercion and permit them to join freely the system of giving. But beyond the minimum it is demoralizing. Risks are inevitable. Welfare services exert a constant, seductive and erosive pressure on the marriage and working habits of the poor.[39] Entrepreneurial knowledge cannot be reproduced in a government plan.[40] Only individuals can be original, and ownership is the key to this. It exposes one both to the risks and the benefits. The trouble about socialism is that it is an insurance against risks, it assumes that we know most of what we need to know, whereas capitalism pre-supposes uncertainty, optimism and faith; rational calculation is not enough. Indeed capitalism involves a world ruled by morality and providence.[41] The invisible hand has returned to justify an otherwise incomprehensible universe in which chance and luck are needed so that there can be an area of freedom which is the condition of creativity.[42] Gilder holds that many public sector and non-profit jobs are well worth subsidizing so long as it is realized that they are dependent on the productive labour of others.[43] He is not a monetarist. He does not approve the fighting of inflation by monetary contraction, and is prepared to contemplate huge public deficits.[44] The crucial question in a capitalist country is the quality and quantity of investment by the rich. A tax increase does not greatly affect their consumption, but it does affect their calculations on saving and investment.[45] It is not the greater consumption or repair, duplication and expansion of existing capital plants which is the point, but its replacement with new and better ones.[46] This is what Schumpeter called 'creative destruction'.[47] Socialist governments are doomed to support the past because creativity is unpredictable and uncontrollable. Scientific establishments, indeed, also resist change. Even voluntary wage and price controls mostly penalize rapidly growing and changing corporations. Indeed new developments do not usually emerge from large enterprises; they tend to consolidate and rationalize. Finally the attempt of the Welfare State to deny, suppress and plan away the dangers and uncertainties of our lives violates the nature of man.[48]

Notice that we cannot get away from the basic beliefs about the nature of man in all these discussions, whether it is open or unavowed. Creativity and risk taking are certainly characteristic of man; but so is the need for basic securities, not least for family life. Efficiency in maximizing economic resources has to be balanced against humanity. Our present social welfare economies have not got the balance right, or we should not have so many million citizens condemned to poverty and powerlessness. The command economies have not got it right for they suffocate human beings in a 'big brother' atmosphere. The pure theory of a laissez-faire society is a pipe dream which no one will allow to be implemented. We are in search of an advanced industrial society which makes a better job of balancing efficiency and humanity. Gilder's praise of creativity is a useful antidote against the defensive clinging to obsolescence which characterizes our society, where millions of people value the new found relative affluence which came to them in the years 1948–73, and cling to it by demanding policies which will erode it. They do this because we have not devised a society which cushions people who are, or would be, particularly hit by technological change, and in particular a society which harnesses the qualities of the technologically unskilled; that is to say half our working population. But Gilder's picture of the necessary conditions for creativity is too simple. Japan, for instance, which has had the most dynamic economic success in the last decades, has also the most developed welfare state in the shape of the least unemployment, least crime, most extensive education and longest expectation of life in the industrial world.[49] Gilder's picture of the altruism of capitalism has a touch of truth in it (remember the Quaker virtues which I mentioned earlier), but if we ask who is nearer the truth in the matter of motivation, Adam Smith or George Gilder, Adam Smith is clearly the winner.

I have been dealing with moral arguments in connection with capitalism, and have noted that providence as an invisible hand is still around. There are, however, more latent and explicit religious references in the discussions. President Reagan has more than once referred to the USA as 'A city set upon a hill'. This is a phrase from a sermon by John Winthrop, one of the Pilgrim Fathers, on board ship for Massachusetts in 1620. He referred to ridding oneself from sin within. Ronald Reagan uses it against liberals and communists. Other more explicit attempts to link the free enterprise system with the Bible are made. Jerry Falwell, the leader of the Moral Majority, finds it clearly outlined in the book of Proverbs. On the Roman Catholic side it has been said that the principle of subsidiarity, introduced by Pius XI into the encyclical *Quadragesimo Anno* in 1931[50] leads to private enterprise and a free market, which is just as far fetched a deduction as that of Falwell from Proverbs.[51] It is said that opposition to free competition is hedonistic since the real objection is that it makes life too arduous, and that a dose of Christian responsibility and the Protestant work ethic of self-help is what is needed today. A Christian emphasis on rules has also been held to lead to an approval of the Gold Standard, and the removal of discretion over monetary policy in favour of following a rule. I referred to this in the second chapter.

Much of the Christian support comes from evangelical 'twice born' Christians. All three candidates in the last Presidential election in the USA, Ronald Reagan, Jimmy Carter and John Anderson, were 'twice born' Christians. However, evangelicals are as divided there on these matters as they are in Britain. Some of them take no interest in any of these issues on the grounds that the parousia is imminent, others use sophisticated political lobbying techniques in favour of a mixture of 'puritan' morality, laissez-faire economies and nationalism. Billy Graham is now said to regret any tendency to confuse the kingdom of God with the American way of life. I have seen an estimate which makes 20% of evangelicals in the USA on the left, 31% in the centre and 37% on the right (the remainder did not identify themselves; if they were non-political that would in practice mean that they are on the right). So the religious right is not completely identified with the radical right.

In the last resort the spirituality of the radical right has been well characterized by Peter Selby[52] as an individualism which finds success in terms of personal rather than corporate achievements; which holds that unless everyone bears the consequences of his own action it is feather bedding; that unless virtues have their personal rewards they will not be practised; that man in collectives is depraved, so that 'organized labour' destroys freedom rather than promotes creativity; that has no place for human solidarity; that accepts public provision only as a last resort when voluntarism has failed; and that regards compassion, faithfulness and generosity as leisure time activities. It is a spirituality which I regard as gravely defective, and it is very far from that emerging within the ecumenical movement (which has been the most significant feature of church history in this century), and which is the main concern of the next chapter.

4

The Trend to the Left in Twentieth-Century
Social Theology

The focus of this chapter is what in contrast to the new radical
right might well be called the new ecumenical left, as expressed
in the thinking of the World Council of Churches, the Roman
Catholic Church, and the more radical left of liberation theology,
which straddles both. However to begin with I propose to refer
once more to the Christian Social Union in England, as represented by Scott Holland, which might be thought of as the
old left, and to consider the social teaching of the Dutch neo-
Calvinist school which has had some recent influence on
evangelical social thinking in this country, and which has had
the effect of making it more critical and in that sense left.

1. Scott Holland's social theology

It is worth looking briefly at Scott Holland's social theology because of its influence on William Temple and many others of his
generation, and through William Temple on the early stages of
the Life and Work side of the ecumenical movement. Scott
Holland was Chairman of the committee of the CSU from 1899,
and editor of its journal *The Commonwealth* from its inception in
1896 until his death, and of a handbook, *Our Neighbours*, which
it published in 1911. More radical Christians criticized the CSU
as being too bland, and apt to cover up serious issues with cloudy
generalizations. But we have seen reason to believe that their
own stance was characterized by an inadequate understanding
of the basic problems of any economic order. I am interested
in the general legacy left by Scott Holland to social theology,
as a very representative figure in a body which had a good

deal of influence in the Church of England and beyond.[1]

He was clear on the need to get beyond a Christian ethic of purely private virtues and personal holiness. He accepted the need for state intervention, as did Steward Headlam and the Christian socialists of the late nineteenth century, unlike F. D. Maurice. The influence of Hegel as transmitted through T. H. Green can be traced here. Scott Holland saw that good laws themselves do not produce interior personal renewal, though they do assist citizens to behave in ways which might help rather than hinder that renewal. To put it at its most negative, state actions can 'hinder hindrances to the good life'. Good social laws set free our corporate selves from narrow selfishness. He did not accept the philosophy attached to laissez-faire, and spotted that the system of competition actually pre-supposes a delicate web of commitment to human co-operation underlying it. An indication of the flavour of his thought can be obtained from a passage in *Our Neighbours*:

> Capital and Labour should be but two sides of a single fact . . . They need not be in opposition, but only in antithesis . . . There must be some foothold (sc. in industry and society) for a man outside and beyond his wage . . . For industry is a fellowship. It is not a blind collision of opposing interests . . . So both capital and labour fall together under the regulative control of one supreme authority (sc. the state) which can assert over both the moral and human claims of the whole community.[2]

The basically valid insights here need to be distilled from the rather optimistic view of a conflict-free community and a neutral state smoothing out disharmonies in order that fellowship may have full sway. It is a legacy of the belief in progress which was so much part of the air the nineteenth century breathed. It is these insights which one finds in William Temple, sometimes in the same language, until the middle 1930s, after which, largely under the influence of Reinhold Niebuhr, his understanding of the endemic conflicts of interest in human society deepened. The force of Scott Holland's insights is a recovery of the inherently corporate nature of human life and its need to be expressed in the fundamental economic and political structures of society, a fraternity within which the polarities of liberty and equality have to be contained. Social theology should articulate this, not merely for the authenticity of the faith itself and the practice of the church, but for the good of the whole body politic. This recovery was needed because of the individualistic nature of the dominant intellectual trends of Christian social thought which followed the collapse of the Christian social tradition at the end of the seventeenth century, and which in any case had become so inadequate in face of the entirely new type of civilization in the history of the world produced by the Industrial Revolution.

The importance of this excursus into the CSU is that the legacy of this kind of social theology grew in the course of this century, William Temple being one of its foremost exponents, and played its part in the establishment of the Welfare State and the broad consensus referred to as Butskellism, as well as contributing a good deal to the ecumenical movement. This last has now become more radical, as we shall see very shortly, whilst the new radical right, as we have already seen, has called it all into question in favour of a return to a competitive individualist outlook wherein personal benevolence is a markedly subordinate option.

2. Dutch neo-Calvinism and its social theology

Recent years have seen a development in evangelical social thought which was unknown until recently.[3] Whilst there were some notable evangelicals in the nineteenth century who had a social conscience, one thinks of the Clapham Sect, of Shaftesbury and General Booth as examples, they had no social theology. Now there is a change, under the pressures which have created the ecumenical movement (of which evangelicals have been suspicious). The most dramatic change has been among a minority of Protestants in Latin America who have joined with a larger minority of Roman Catholics in developing liberation theology, to which I shall refer later.

The roots of evangelicalism are diverse. There is the Lutheran tradition, with its characteristic doctrine of the Two Realms, which is not indigenously represented in Britain. There is the Anabaptist element of the left wing of the Reformation, which is but sparsely represented in contemporary Britain. And there is the Calvinist tradition, which has been quite powerfully represented and is still a significant element in Britain. It is to this, the third root of their theology, that evangelicals tend to turn for the basis of a social theology. Since that element of it never developed in Britain attention has turned to Holland, where a neo-Scholastic Calvinist social theology developed in the later nineteenth century. What are its possibilities?[4]

Abraham Kuyper (1837–1920) is the most important figure in the development of neo-Calvinism. He was a theologian and statesman. He was in fact Prime Minister from 1901–4, being the founder of the Anti-Revolutionary Party. He was also the founder of the Free University of Amsterdam on a Calvinist Confessional basis, the founder of a Christian daily paper, *Do Standaard*, and he deeply influenced the Dutch Christian labour movement. His theology was developed particularly by Herman Dooyewaard (1894–1977) in what was called the philosophy of the Cosmonic Idea. We need not delve into that for our present purpose which is concerned with social theology. Here there are three concepts to note: (1) that of the Calling; (2) that of the Anti-Thesis and common grace; (3) that of the architectonical critique of the social order. All of them derive, as one would expect in Calvinism, from a stress on the sovereignty of God.

The concept of the Calling has been much discussed in studies of the Reformation, and especially of the relation between the Protestant ethic and the spirit of capitalism, and this is not the occasion to add to them. Suffice it to say that stress on one's calling led to a stress on the daily work of the world as the place where a Christian is to respond to God, and that there is no higher place in which to do so, certainly not by taking 'religious' vows and living in a monastery or nunnery. Further, part of this obedience is that of occupying an office, the faithful carrying out of the duties of which is also a calling from God. Thus the institutions of society have their place under God, expressed by Kuyper and Dooyewaard as the 'principle of sphere sovereignty'.[5] Between these spheres – family, school, workshop, trade union, church – there is a basic equality, and in each of them we are responsible to God; none of them, especially neither the church nor the state, should try to subordinate the other spheres to it. The term 'sovereignty' in the phrase 'sphere sovereignty' does not mean that the sphere is autonomous but refers to the sovereignty of God over each sphere. He requires, for instance, faithful love in marriage, stewardship in economic matters, and justice in the state. There should be a respect for the God-given authority of each sphere lest society fall into anarchy. Nevertheless Kuyper requires the state to intervene to bring back the other spheres to their proper task if they go astray from it. I do not see how these two positions with regard to the state fit together. And what if the state abuses its powers? Here the teaching is uncertain, for neo-Calvinism combines a democratic with a conservative stance. Within the state, however, when the democratic note is applied to stewardship in the sphere of industry it can lead to thoughts of the common responsibility of managers, workers and shareholders for an undertaking, including workers' share in management (or *mitbestimmung* as the Germans call it); and it certainly excludes the thought of ownership of labour as if it were just the same as land or capital as a factor of production.

The concept of Anti-Thesis arises out of the situation, different from that of the Reformation, in which Christians live in a society with others who do not share their faith. Kuyper holds that certain fundamental moral requirements are laid down by God for the spheres, especially the state (he cannot talk of Natural Law, though Calvin might have done) such that if it systematically abuses its powers it becomes 'revolutionary'. Note the very unusual sense in which the term is used. In that case those who are able to lead the nation should resist, for having authority is no more 'holy' than being subject to authority. Was not Christ among us as one who served? The Anti-Thesis is the radical distinction between the kingdom of God and the kingdom of darkness, but this is not the same as the distinction between Christian and non-Christian for Christians, too, are sinful. That is why God's common grace extends to all; his sunshine and rain is not restricted to Christians. All are called to co-operate in the spheres, even though Christians are tempted to withdraw into their own separate communities. Kuyper founded many separate Christian organizations but expected them to play an active role in society under God's common grace. A Christian political party is not meant to be a self-centred place for Christians, nor a missionary body, but a place from which to move into the political sphere to work for justice in it.[6]

Kuyper's third concept, the architectonic critique of society, led him to make what appear to be very drastic criticisms of it. 'Where poor and rich stand over against each other Jesus never chose his place at the side of the rich.' Between the kingdom of God and capitalism 'there is an absolute contradiction'. However, the conclusions he drew from this were modest. The state must intervene in the cause of justice, with due respect for the autonomy of each sphere, in order to make possible the fulfilment of the Calling within it. It must intervene today, for instance, both in respect of inflation and unemployment, both of which impose serious injustices on certain persons and groups, particularly those who cannot fight back, whether in the developed or the poorer nations. The architectonic critique must be applied today to the spheres in our society, and especially to governments, lest they give in to the most powerful pressure groups, and adopt the line of least resistance instead of bold and imaginative measures.

The strength of this neo-Calvinism is that it denies the otherworldliness of so much Puritan and evangelical theology by rooting the sovereignty of God in a doctrine of creation which obliges Christians to take a responsible part in society. That is why evangelicals can turn to it for a social theology. Spurgeon, for instance, an outstanding British Calvinist contemporary of Kuyper, confined his stress on the sovereignty of God to a soteriology of individual salvation. But apart from this there are many difficulties in this position. What are the spheres and what are their boundaries? Kuyper and Dooyewaard rejected racism, but many South Africans have regarded sphere sovereignty as a basis for apartheid, as many Lutherans under Hitler made race an order of creation. Members of Kuyper's own family joined the Dutch Nazi party. How does one decide whether the state is infringing the autonomy of the spheres, or if they are infringing one another's autonomy? When is a revolution against God-given authority justifiable? Calvinists in the past have supported revolts against the authorities. That is how both the Netherlands and the USA were founded. Yet Dutch neo-Calvinist thought today seems ultra-cautious by comparison. Indeed the application of the category of revolutionary and non-revolutionary is hard to see. A government which systematically misuses its power is in this terminology revolutionary and to oppose it is non-revolutionary. If then, Chief Gatcha Buthelezi, who is surely a responsible leader, were to lead the Zulus to resist the South African government he would be non-revolutionary, yet most Calvinist Afrikaaners would oppose him and support the government.

Neo-Calvinism has been thought out in an isolationist spirit. It was formed in the last years of the pre-ecumenical age. In spite of its talk of a plural society it has tended to cultivate an isolationist spirit both within the nation and against other confessional traditions. It exhibits a weakness common to many theologies of society, high abstraction with vague practical content. It would greatly benefit from more ecumenical contacts for mutual correction, and it is just the extent and depth of these in Holland in recent years which have weakened it so much in that country. Its positive points, on the calling and a common grace, have been expressed as well or better elsewhere; its architectonic critique has not produced any analysis more searching than others of modern society, nor has it shown any notable percipience in spotting passing intellectual fads, in spite of its polemics against humanism and liberalism. Its polemics against humanism ignore the Christian elements latent in the humanism of Western society, which can often be an ally of causes which Christians may wish to promote in that plural society. Its penchant for separate Christian political parties and trade unions is a source of confusion and fissiparousness. It will not do as it stands as a social theology.

3. The social theology of the World Council of Churches

The tendency to the left in the economic, social and political thinking of the World Council of Churches dates from the earliest days of the ecumenical movement, simply because that movement has been concerned not only for the unity of the church but also its renewal. Concern for renewal involves a concern for its effective influence in human society, and that soon raises questions as to whether that society is to be taken as it stands as a place for Christian witness, or whether the witness does not call in question features of the society in the light of the gospel. Two world wars, two serious economic depressions, the experience of vicious totalitarian movements, and the opposition of so much of the Third World against the hegemony of white people and the expressions of white racism, come to mind at once as reasons why a critique of twentieth-century society has been called for. Hence 'Life and Work' was as prominent as 'Faith and Order' in the preparatory years of the ecumenical movement, when it was largely Western orientated, and so it has continued since the World Council of Churches was formed at Amsterdam in 1948. Since then it has become much more global.[7]

The Stockholm Conference of 1925 was the first international ecumenical conference on social ethics. Apart from the question of German war guilt, a concern which had not yet died down and had to be faced, the conference in broad terms found itself divided between a more Anglo-Saxon liberal theology with respect to building the kingdom of God and a more European continental confessional Protestant rejection of any such idea. But there was considerable agreement on what was needed to repair the ravages of the First World War and the disasters of the peace which followed it for the conference to arrive at the conviction that 'doctrine divides but service unites'. Years later it was to be found that the opposite is also true. Every church in the ecumenical world condemned racism as a doctrine, but controversy arose over the actions decided upon by the World Council of Churches to give practical effect to the verbal condemnation. The only churches to leave the WCC have done so on this issue.

Stockholm showed sufficient promise for the decision to be made to keep its organizational machinery in being, and this became the 'Life and Work' side of the ecumenical movement. The next major step was the Oxford Conference on Church, Community and State (1937), called in the shadow of the mass unemployment in the Western world following upon the Wall Street crash of 1929, the rise of totalitarian Nazi and Fascist movements, and the growth of re-armament. It had a substantial theological input, of a quality never since bettered and perhaps not equalled. Its third section was devoted to the economic order, and its report built upon the traditions of Christian social theology with which this book began but, largely under the influence of Reinhold Niebuhr, put its criticisms of the market economy in a less idealistic framework.[8] Both he and Temple were members of the drafting committee. Its fundamental teaching has not been superseded, though the first Assembly of the newly formed WCC at Amsterdam in 1948 dealt with the issues of capitalism and socialism with more precision.

By the time of the formation of the Council the World War had been succeeded by the Cold War. Being so much a Western body, and withal largely financed from the USA, it would have been only too easy to line up the churches with the West in the Cold War, but that was not done. Thanks to the years of ecumenical consultation and reflection put in beforehand under the leadership of men like Dr J. H. Oldham,[9] a theological basis for criticism of the economic, social and political order was achieved in the concept of 'the responsible society'.[10]

A responsible society is one where freedom is the freedom of men who acknowledge responsibility to justice and public order and where those who hold political authority or economic power are responsible for its exercise to God and to the people whose welfare is affected by it.

These criteria were and are applicable in different ways to all societies, including both sides in the Cold War.

The WCC developed at the time of rapid political decolonialization after the war of 1939–45. The WCC began an examination of the rapid social change which was being brought about by this and by social and technological factors. Continuing structures of economic power and colonial dependence were revealed, and from the third Assembly at New Delhi the issues of the relations between rich and poor countries have been prominent. Problems arising out of this are hard to resolve. On the one hand the obligation of the First World to establish preferably international institutions, including taxes, to further the development of the Third World is stressed, which diminishes national sovereignty; whilst on the other the importance of national sovereignty and independence is stressed with respect to the Third World, together with self-reliance, as against dependence on the 'West'. Dissatisfaction with this dependence was expressed in the 1966 Geneva Conference on 'Christians in the Technical and Social Revolutions of our Time', which was an attempt to do for the ecumenical concerns in this area what the Oxford Conference had done in 1937, but this time on a truly ecumenical scale, geographically and confessionally, with the West no longer able to set the agenda.[11] Of the members, 47% came from the Third World. The result was a radical conference, which shook some of the membership from the Western countries, particularly the USA, but which was broadly endorsed by the fourth Assembly of the WCC at Uppsala two years later in 1968. (Geneva had been an unofficial study conference.) Following this Assembly, work began on the whole problem of man's freedom and fulfilment in societies which were everywhere on the move, consciously future orientated, and unwilling to drift on under the dominance of others, but wanting to take much greater responsibility for it themselves. Out of this study came the concept of the just, participatory and sustainable society with which the WCC has been working between the fifth Nairobi Assembly of 1975 and the sixth in Vancouver in 1983. It has replaced the responsible society, which had seemed to many, whether rightly or wrongly, too tied to the Western type of political democracy and a mixed economy, and is certainly more specific and comprehensive. At Nairobi two items, militarism and trans-national corporations, were added to the agenda. Most of this work until recently was carried out by the 'Church and Society' department of the WCC under Dr Paul Abrecht, but it has now expanded far beyond that department. Indeed 'Church and Society' has been so occupied in recent years with the urgent issues involved in the development of nuclear energy, and the ethos of natural and applied science, that its small resources have given it little time for other issues.

This is the reason why I have not found a great deal of help in recent WCC studies on the theme of this book. The last major Study Conference was at the Massachusetts Institute of Technology in 1979, which was in some ways a successor to Oxford and Geneva. Its theme was 'Faith, Science and the Future', and reflected the recent preoccupations of the department on 'Church and Society'. The economic side was small and had little to say.[12] The last effort on the economic front was a small international consultation at Zurich in 1978 on 'Political Economy and Ethics' which left a whole series of questions to be explored further.[13] To put it concisely, in a global consultation the constituency of the WCC is for the most part highly critical of Western economies (not without reason), aware that the polar opposite command economies are not working well, and talks very generally and unrealistically about alternatives. It moves fairly rapidly away from economic to political considerations, where again it thinks unrealistically. There has been in addition a division between First and Third World personnel which has not helped the grappling with basic economic problems. Many of the First World members have been preoccupied with the Limits to Growth issues since the first report of the Club of Rome. Sustainability quickly came on to the agenda, at a Consultation at Bucharest in 1974.[14] An interesting paradox has arisen. The Third World (and indeed the Second or Marxist World) has been too sceptical of this. It has regarded pre-occupation with issues of ecology and the exhaustion of natural resources as a device of the wealthy world to keep the rest in their place. It has been too sceptical, whereas the First World has taken them too seriously; at least the people from it who attend ecumenical conferences have done so. They are in economic positions which lead them to read the quality newspapers, and it is among such people that the churches are strongest. It is these who were most misled by the Club of Rome's first report. The working-class movements were never impressed. However, a more balanced perspective is now developing on the issue.

What of participation? There is no question that participation in decisions which vitally affect one is necessary if a person is to express his full humanity, and that throughout history and today many millions are just pushed around by others. For instance until the last century most upper and middle-class people regarded the working classes as a different species, not suitable to share in decision making. Self-reliant development from the bottom upwards is needed. However structures of participation and representation in advanced and complex societies, whether political, economic, social or industrial, will be far from easy to achieve if decisions are to be adequately informed, made in time when change is rapid, and if minorities are to be respected. Some of the discussions seem to imply that decisions can be made by local grass-roots meetings who will arrive at a consensus and there will be no minorities. Furthermore one detects at times a middle-class assumption behind the talk of 'conscientization' of the millions on the margins of existence (who Marxists call the *lumpen* proletariat), that they know what the unprivileged ought to think. It is allied with a tendency to think of the poor as a much more unified class than they are, at least in the Western world and, one suspects, in others. A recent Consultation on Ecumenical Perspectives in Political Ethics elaborates a conception of 'the People',[15] which appears to mean all those not at present running the government in Third World countries. It assumes that they are a unified body but are not yet organized in a participatory way. How would this apply to Zimbabwe, as an example?

An unresolved dichotomy runs through the documents. The kingdom of God is seen as something to hope for, whilst the New Testament understanding that it is already a reality and we are citizens of it is ignored. It is the absence of this one side of the two-fold understanding of the kingdom which leads to utopianism in the documents. We are told that the kingdom of God cannot be converted into a political ideology to be realized historically, that politics must not be sacralized, and neither must any economic system. But we are also told that a Christian political ethic 'does not simply work for a "transfer of power" or even the "empowerment of the people", but rather for the transformation of political power under the image of the cross of Jesus Christ, the suffering Messiah'. It is said that the wisdom of the people is the one sound foundation for ethical work, and that they are to liberate themselves from all forms of bondage and form a new community working for the common good. The people is to recover its roots and articulate its present sufferings in the search for the messianic kingdom. This language is much below the level of political and economic analysis which has usually characterized the ecumenical movement. So is the sentiment one finds creeping from time to time into the document that we should move from self-interest to social concern or to altruism as the basis of economic activity.[16] About this I add no more to what has already been discussed in previous chapters.

Nevertheless despite these criticisms[17] the general stance emerging from World Council of Churches assemblies, conferences and consultations is persuasive and radical. It emphases over and over again that the churches need to express their solidarity with the struggles of the poor against poverty and exploitation, and to establish a new relationship with the poor inside the churches.[18] How this is to be done, and what in detail it means, involves differences of opinion on which more needs to be said in the last two chapters. But it is clear that the general stance is an ecumenism of the left, as compared with the traditional stances of the churches down the centuries.[19]

4. The move to the left in Roman Catholic social theology

There has been a movement to the Left in Roman Catholic social theology parallel to that of the ecumenical movement, but developing later; in fact with Pope John XXIII and the Second Vatican Council.[20] We have already seen that Roman Catholic social theology made a new start with Leo XIII's Encyclical *Rerum Novarum* in 1891. It had faded out in the course of the eighteenth century, and the nineteenth had seen the Roman Catholic position epitomized in Pius IX's Syllabus of Errors of 1864. which was a blast against almost everything going on in the Western world around him at the time. Leo XIII moved from the negatives of Pius IX to the adumbration of a new social order. Because he was so tied to the past he saw more easily through the pretensions of nineteenth century capitalist societies than the leaders of the Protestant and Anglican churches who were more bound up with it, and this led him to go to the past and call for a revival of Thomism.[21] He distanced himself from the *ancien régime* and the aristocratic order, still largely based on landed property, but drew upon mediaeval social teaching which stressed the organic, and indeed hierarchical, nature of society, the relative autonomy of the natural order (but with the church in the background to guide it), and the need to pursue the common good and to protect the poor. Roman Catholic teaching continued on these general lines until about 1950. Leo XIII was not taken in by the ideology of laissez-faire, and wished to promote active policies which would improve the lot of the workers. Unfortunately he showed no more understanding of the problems of the economic system, as exposed by the development of economics, than did the Christian socialists, although by then it was a well-developed science, in the process of shedding its utilitarian philosophical associations through the development of marginal analysis, of which the Austrian School was the pioneer. This was discussed in the second chapter. But Leo did not draw socialist conclusions from his critique of the market economy, because of his inherited teaching on private property. Here he was more absolute even than mediaeval teaching, perhaps without realizing it, being influenced by Lockean teaching; for in *Rerum Novarum* private property becomes a metaphysical right based on man's labour by which 'he appropriates that part of physical nature which he has cultivated'.[22] This right to private ownership must be preserved inviolate, and also the right to inherit it, although the state may modify its use. This teaching is echoed in Pius XI's Encyclical, *Quadragesimo Anno*, issued in 1931 to commemorate that of Leo XIII.[23] Such a doctrine of private property is in fact more absolute than that of Locke,[24] and has now been repudiated by John Paul II in his recent Encyclical *Laborem Exercens* (1981) where he says, 'the right to private property is subordinate to the right to common use, to the fact that goods are meant for everyone', which is a return to St Thomas Aquinas.[25]

Some of Leo's criticisms of the market system arise from interventions in it by the state, which prevent it working according to its theory. He did not understand this because he did not understand the theory of the market, but even if he had he could not have approved of the market contract as the sole link between men as producers and consumers. As it is he assumes artlessly that because capital and labour are necessary to each other there must be capitalist and labouring classes.[26] However he specifically criticizes the labour contract in favour of a minimum wage capable of supplying the essentials of life for a worker and his family.[27] *Rerum Novarum* seems basically an attempt to adapt a mediaeval theory to a new type of society, an industrial one, without the necessary analytical tools. It rejects laissez-faire, secularization, equalitarianism, socialism and parliamentary democracy, and seems to favour what we used to call a 'corporate state' when Mussolini controlled Italy. This impression is increased by *Quadragesimo Anno* which has several phrases, reportedly added by Pius XI himself, which seem particularly to endorse it.[28]

There was some shift in this teaching under Pius XII at the end of the Second World War. At this time the thought of Jacques Maritain was very influential.[29] An acceptance of modern Western democracy and of a reformed or 'social welfare' capitalism was a keynote of the Christian democratic parties of Western Europe,[30] a kind of third way between capitalism and socialism. However a more marked shift came with the Papacy of John XXIII. His Encyclical *Pacem in Terris* (1963) gave the green light for a more open approach to Marxism than the hitherto blank opposition.[31] The Pastoral Constitution of the

Second Vatican Council, *Gaudium et Spes*, showed a weakening of the old, rationalistic, purely deductive ethic on economic matters. The general principles it enunciated were much more related to factual analysis, in the light of both of which responsible pastoral action was to be based. After the Council Paul VI's Encyclical *Populorum Progressio* (1968) continued this trend, as did his letter to Cardinal Roy of 1971, *Octogesima Adveniens*, once more commemorating *Rerum Novarum*. The first hints, rather than openly says, that multi-national corporations were becoming more powerful than some governments,[32] and that the power of the State or some international authority would be needed as a counterweight. Previously one reason for the anti-socialist line taken by Roman Catholic teaching had been suspicion of the over-weening State, but this was now modified. There is also a cautious reference to legitimate revolutionary movements. In *Octogesima Adveniens* Paul VI recognized that it was out of a concern for Christian values that many Christians had become socialists,[33] and that socialism took many forms and not necessarily the monolithic one of its stereotype. Marxism also was more than a rival world-view to be totally opposed, and can be appraised at a lesser level as a theory of society.

The year 1968 saw the most radical statement of Roman Catholic social theology in the report of the second conference of Latin American Bishops (CELAM) at Medellin in Columbia. This was a response to the growing social and political ferment in Latin America, and the rise of liberation theology, to which I shall turn in the next section. In the same year as *Octogesima Adveniens* the post-Council Synod of Bishops at Rome issued an important document, *Justice in the World* which, in the spirit of Medellin, stressed social and not just personal sin; sin embodied in collective structures of oppression and dehumanization. It said that the Christian understanding of salvation includes social salvation or liberation from these oppressive structures. Lastly we come to John Paul II's recent Encyclical *Laborem Exercens* (1981), which is yet another commemoration of *Rerum Novarum*, though its tone is very different. One might say that it comes now to a non-Marxist but socialist view of society. It stresses the need for solidarity *of* the workers and *with* the workers, and solidarity with the poor.[34] It affirms the priority of labour over capital[35] and that ownership, whether private or public, must express this.

Socialization cannot be excluded. Rigid capitalism is unaccept-able. Workers should be co-owners and co-policy makers; and over-all planning of the economy is required,[36] though not only by the government.

The third conference of CELAM at Puebla in 1979 marked a slight back-tracking from Medellin because the leading Latin American theologians and reforming bishops were excluded from it through dubious intrigues beforehand.[37] It was a striking illustration of the differences within the Roman Catholic Church concerning acceptance of Vatican II and post-Council teaching. One must hazard a guess that there can be no going back to the position of a generation ago, and that the shift to the left as com-pared with that will remain even as the inevitable difficulties it both reveals and causes are faced. However all churches have implicit worries about alienating the middle classes from whom, at least in the Western world, their main numerical and financial support comes.[38]

5. *The radical left of liberation theology*

The more radical side of the ecumenical left shades into libera-tion theology which, although originating in Latin America only about twenty years ago, is having a growing influence in Asia and Africa (though at first it seemed alien there), and also in the First World. In a sense it is the *new* left in theology. To understand it properly it would be necessary to consider the post-1945 political theology in Western Europe, which many of the Latin American exponents of liberation theology met in periods of study in Europe. They criticized it as in the last resort sitting on the fence rather than committing itself to the cause of the poor, because of an 'eschatological reserve' which raised questions against all social, political and economic orders. It is not that liberation theologians have any intention of equating a liberated society with the fulfilment of the gospel. Rather they hold that one can-not get from the Bible an analysis of twentieth-century society in order to know how to implement Biblical faith; one needs a 'science' for this. That science is Marxism.[39] However even to understand the Bible one must first be actively committed to the cause of the poor; then one turns to the Bible for illumination on the Christian faith and life and, further enlightened, one continues one's active struggles with, and not only for, the poor. The process is sometimes called a dialectical relation between praxis and theory, by those who like to use the Hegelian-Marxist term dialectical, and the Marxist term praxis for practice. I prefer to use the term reciprocal, and this might be acceptable to many of the liberation theologians, to express the relation between thought and practice. It is a new way of doing theology and biblical studies in that it takes seriously the social context of theological studies and of the reader of the Bible. In particular it works with a 'one kingdom' view of the Christian life, in which Yahweh's deliverance of the people of God at the Exodus and the saving work of Christ, are seen as paradigms of his general actions in history in the *praxis* of which Christians must be involved.

But what kind of Marxism does it turn to? Marxism is a growingly plural phenomenon, as indeed Christianity is. Is it the early or late Marx (if there is a significant difference between the two, which itself is disputed)? Is it Leninism? Trotskyism? Maoism? It is certainly not Stalinism, which few approve of, and therefore are not likely to follow Althusser; more likely Adorno and the Frankfurt School. Or Gramsci? Both Gutierrez, perhaps the leading theologian of liberation, and the pacifist Bishop Helder Camara of Reçife in north-east Brazil have said that Marx should be to theologians today what Aristotle was to St Thomas Aquinas. This assertation that Marxism is the science of society, unearthing general laws of social change, seems always to be assumed as obvious and not argued. It has in fact to be seriously questioned. In practice the liberation theologians take what they want in a very broad way from Marxism to give them confidence in action with the poor, often partially demythologizing it. In some way or other, however, they hold that the Marxist analysis points to the way the future can be built and is, indeed, struggling to be born. The weakness of Marxism in understanding the person and in coping with death does not worry liberation theologians. They have hardly yet got round to seeing its weakness in dealing with ecological issues, or feminism, or in understanding nationalism. It is the ongoing search for a science of the social future which is their concern. There are good grounds for holding that such a science does not exist, and logically cannot be arrived at. To this I shall return. However on this basis the concepts of ideology and utopia are brought into service. Ideologies are to mobilize visions to enable those committed to a revolutionary change in society to carry out their historical projects. Revolutionary does not necessarily mean violent, though it may do; rather it means rapid and thorough. Utopia is often used in the same sense as ideology, though sometimes in a minimal sense, as by Rubem Alves who says utopianism is 'not a belief in the possibility of a perfect society, but rather the belief in the non-necessity of *this* imperfect order',[40] a sentiment with which all but extreme traditionalists can agree. I myself think that all Christians, faced with the eschatological challenge of the gospels, should agree. There is thus a spectrum within liberation theology. At one end there is this profound but restrained statement, together with reflections on the need to maximize the human possibilities and minimize the human cost of social change; at the other end there are demands for the immediate realization of a totally new society, without delay or intermediate stages.[41]

In detail I do not think liberation theology can be of much help to us.[42] What is important about it is that in its analysis it not only stresses commitment to the poor, but it raises critical questions about the church itself. The church likes to think of herself as impartially preaching gospel truth and giving gospel advice to all classes and groups. Yet how far is the church herself part of the structures of oppression? Also under the inspiration of liberation theology basic communities (*communidades de base*) of liturgical and social life have grown up, particularly in Brazil, where there are said to be over 100,000 of them and that they are the real growing point of the church, although they are only loosely related to parochial structures. These two points lead directly to the question of the prophetic role of the church, to which I turn in the next chapter.

5

Problems of Prophecy

Functional sociologists classify religion with law as the means by which societies produce the sanctions which enable them to cohere and hold together.[1] A generic study of religion shows that there is much evidence to support this connection; and the Christian religion is no exception. Considering its origin in the ministry of an itinerant charismatic figure operating on the margin of the institutions of society,[2] and preaching a gospel of which a radical kingdom of God was a central feature, it is surprising that mainstream Christianity, at least from the time of Constantine, has been so overwhelmingly supportive of existing institutions.

All the main Christian confessional traditions took shape against the presumption of a relatively static social order, which for the greater part they supported.[3] Byzantium was the earliest example; the Western Catholic tradition arrived at the conception of the Holy Roman Empire; Lutheranism worked with the Two Realms theory which in effect underpinned the political establishment; Calvinism had a high doctrine of both church and state, but kept the seeds of dynamism in it under fairly firm control; and the Anglican Settlement was a forlorn attempt to recreate Byzantium in sixteenth-century England. Liturgically it is divine preservative activity which is stressed. I am not thinking so much of the prayers in the Book of Common Prayer which teach the divine right of kings, but of the artless way in which the lovely General Thanksgiving, inserted in the Prayer Book of 1662, thanks God for 'creation, *preservation*, and all the blessings of this life'. It was all more plausible before the Industrial Revolution, since when we have been experiencing ever more rapid social change. Even modern liturgies seem not to have caught up with this. One suspects that many worshippers would in many moods not want to thank God for it, but would rather ask him to put a stop to it. Nevertheless a marked devotion to stability is not the best basis for dealing with rapid social change.

Another expression of the alliance of religion with law is the custom of Assize Services in many cathedrals or, instead, an annual service for all connected with law enforcement and the legal profession. This is considered entirely natural, and I have no wish to decry it. Quite the contrary. But it is very rare for those on the receiving end of social institutions to have such a service. The only example known to me is the service in Durham cathedral at the annual Durham Miners' Gala. I am sure that an annual cathedral service for shop stewards would be thought strange, even if more than a handful of shop stewards were prepared to attend. With the legal professions however, there is no difficulty.

There is a vital element in the Judaeo-Christian tradition which does not fit into this easy support of the *status quo*, and which sociologists of religion, particularly functional sociologists, do not find it easy to incorporate into their analyses. I refer to the prophetic tradition. Traces of the prophetic tradition are found at least from the early days of the monarchy, and its critical role developed rapidly. Christians are also heir to it, for there are many prophetic elements in the teaching of Jesus, and indeed, in Mark 6.4 he indirectly appropriates the title. It is not surprising, therefore, that there are frequent complaints that the strong support of the churches of those in authority means that the church is not prophetic. There are demands that it should be, and in particular that clergy and ministers should be. We need to look at the prophetic tradition in its context, and ask how far it can be translated into our situation. We need also to consider whether there is any difference between what is possible for the church collectively and Christians individually in the task of being prophetic.

1. Prophecy in the Old Testament

The prophets of the Old Testament were moral innovators. They shared the conviction of the people of Israel that Yahweh had made a covenant with them at the time of Moses so that they were

an elected or chosen people, but greatly modified the understanding of what the covenant and election implied.[4] Popular
religion interpreted it to mean divine favours willy-nilly; the
prophets understood it to mean obedience to certain basic moral
demands, and a greater moral responsibility on those who were
chosen than on those who were not. In doing this they appealed
to the past, to the Mosaic era, when in fact they were reformers,
deepening the understanding of the nature and will of Yahweh.
In II Sam. 12 we find Nathan challenging the King himself on
the grounds of transgression against basic morality by telling him
the story of the ewe lamb, and this led David to convict himself
(by his own moral judgment) of wrongdoing. Later, in I Kings
21, Ahab is sternly rebuked by Elijah for bringing about the
death of Naboth by false accusations in order to take over his
vineyard, conduct which at that time rulers might well have
expected to get away with. The story of the writing prophets is
well-known, through Amos, Hosea, first Isaiah, Micah, Jeremiah
and the rest, and there is no need to repeat it. They spared neither
individuals nor groups, and especially not the administrators of
justice, in terms of basic personal and social ethics. Enough of
their teaching was appropriated by enough of their hearers to
preserve the faith in Yahweh, the God of Israel, at the time of the
exile in 586 BC, when humanly speaking one would have expected
it to die out on the grounds that Yahweh was not as powerful as
the Babylonian gods. The ramnant brought the faith back with
them from exile, and it has preserved believing Jews from then
until the present day.

It was adherence to a basic morality which was required, what
centuries later might well have been called 'Natural Law'. It
was not a morality thought to be peculiar to the Israelites. The
first chapter of Amos and the beginning of the second denounces
Damascus, Gaza, Tyre, Edom, Ammon and Moab for infringing it; and though they had been within the ambit of the Davidic
empire the inhabitants were certainly not adherents of Yahwism.
Indeed the Old Testament does not think that only those who
believe in Yahweh are moral beings. Far from it. It assumes the
reality of moral insight and moral decisions in the life of human
beings, just as it assumes the reality of God, and does not argue
the question. We need to be clear about what it takes for granted,
not least because it is of importance in relating Christian witness

and activity to that of other faiths and ideologies in a plural world. Basic morality is binding on all, and we need to work out its implications together.[5]

The prophets were convinced they had a divine call, although they might accept it only reluctantly, as was the case with Jeremiah.[6] Once accepted, they were convinced they had a divine word from Yahweh. Sometimes the message was received through a vision, more usually by a kind of spirit possession taking control of the prophet, so that the word of the Lord was spoken directly through him. There are many general condemnations of sins such as cheating, greed (including taking interest on a loan),[7] theft, disrespect to parents, adultery and murder. Corruptions of the cult, like sacred prostitution, are condemned.[8] There are specific condemnations of the leaders – prophets, priests and rulers – for taking bribes and other forms of exploitation; but also for putting confidence in military, and indeed any human operation, with respect to the national cause.[9] And then there are many condemnations of other nations because of their arrogance and self-confidence in general, or their treatment of Israel in particular.[10] Amos has already been referred to. Assyria, Babylon and Persia are condemned even though they are unwitting servants of Yahweh in castigating Israel, a role which will be mentioned in the next section. Isaiah 14 has a magnificent taunt song on the state entry of the King of Babylon into Sheol (the underworld, the shadowy place of the departed).

These prophecies usually refer to a transgression that has not yet been punished, but shortly would be. Disaster is seen to be inevitable, and rarely is any hope of amendment expressed.[11] No positive proposals for putting things right are put forward by the prophets, beyond the total reversal of the wrong doing. The culmination of the announcement of disaster was the exile, when in 597 BC most of the leaders, and in 586 all but the *lumpen* proletariat, were carried away into exile in Babylon, and Temple and Monarch alike came to an end.

However the prophets also, as a rule, looked forward to renewal after catastrophe, a new Day of the Lord, a new covenant, or however deliverance was expressed. In this way they gave hope to those whom disaster might have made hopeless, and can be said to be a source of utopian thinking. We may compare this with the saying of Lady Julian of Norwich: 'all shall be well and all manner of things shall be well'.[12] But these hopes were not in fact fulfilled. Whereas the disasters which were prophesied, and interpreted within the Deuteronomic philosophy of history at the time of exile, were fulfilled the promises were not. The return from exile was a far from glorious affair. It took years even to rebuild the walls of Jerusalem.[13] The city was the centre of a very small state, independent for only a brief period, and then the puppet of the major powers and hopelessly involved in their rivalries. Thus it was at the time of Jesus. Out of this disillusion came the development of apocalyptic, which despaired of the present world. Its only message was perseverance in suffering, and its hopes were expressed in the belief that God would shortly intervene directly to clear up the mess, exalt the faithful, and punish the wicked, either in a totally new world or in a total reconstruction of the present one. It would be the end of history, not its fulfilment. It is this kind of thinking which appears to make a more evident transition to the gospels than any other strand of Jewish religious thought, though the connection can be overstated. That is why there has been a strain in Christian thought, largely based on the last book of the New Testament, which has taken over the apocalyptic attitude of the Jewish inter-testamentary period, despairing of the present world and looking to the imminent return of Christ to sort things out. This date has, of course, to be continually pushed forward. I have argued elsewhere that this type of thinking is no use to us today, and must be discarded, and I am not going to repeat that argument now.[14] I am sorry that a mistaken biblicism has allowed it too prominent a place in the new liturgical texts.[15] The task before us is not to deal with problems of apocalyptic today but problems of prophecy, and to that I return. I do not think that it is sensible to ask that the church or individual Christians or groups should be apocalyptic, but it is sensible to ask that they should be prophetic, and to consider what are the implications of being prophetic.

A further element in biblical prophecy is symbolic actions. Notable examples of this are found, for instance, in Jeremiah.[16] We shall have to say something later about their significance today. But these, as well as prophetic words, raise the question of the test of true prophecy. When there are various people claiming to be prophets of the Lord, but not saying the same thing, how does one distinguish true from false prophet? There is a classic confrontation in I Kings 22 between Micaiah-ben-Imlah and four hundred false prophets. Jeremiah has continually to contend with them. The first defence of the prophet was to deny that his rivals had received a genuine word from Yahweh, and that they were corrupt or apostate or both.[17] This was mere assertion. Another appeal was to the prophetic tradition. Anyone announcing smooth things will be a false prophet.[18] Another test was whether his prediction would come true, as in the case of Micaiah-ben-Imlah, but this is no help at the time when an evaluation of rival prophets has to be made.[19] The only place where there is a systematic discussion of the point is Deut. 18.15-22, which promises a series of prophets like Moses, who will be intermediaries for the people with Yahweh, and who will speak words directly from him. However in Deut. 13.1–5 a situation is posited where a prediction of a *false* prophet comes true; and now the test is whether he said 'let us go after other Gods' or not. So a prophet must speak in the name of Yahweh; that is a necessary condition, but it is not a sufficient one, for that he does so is no guarantee in itself that he is a true prophet. None of the suggested criteria solved the problem.

Finally with respect to Old Testament prophecy we may note that it takes place within Israel and Judah conceived as both a people of God, or church, and at the same time a political entity, or state. There is one kingdom, a theocracy; church and state are one. Prophecy effectively began and ended in the period of the monarchy. When Israel lost control of political power classical prophecy ended. After the exile it was but a shadow of what it had been and apocalyptic teaching gained in importance. In the end the priestly tradition ranked the Torah or books of the Law above the prophetic books. There was a belief that prophecy had ceased but that it would return.[20] The arrival of John the Baptist made some ask themselves whether indeed a prophet had appeared in Israel; and his advent heralded that of Jesus.

2. Prophecy in the New Testament

The situation is different in the New Testament. John the Baptist appeared as someone who harked back to the old prophetic role, and Jesus' ministry was clearly in some senses prophetic. It was direct, authoritative and charismatic. The core of it, however, was different from the old tradition of prophecy. Jesus' emphasis was on God's immediate graciousness: the new age was just about to break into the old; indeed its powers were already at work in his ministry. True, that ministry sharpened the issues and demanded a choice. In a sense it was a judgment. But its intention was gracious. Moreover the new age, the kingdom of God, and the bringer of it, Jesus, were very different from traditional expectations. It did not fit in with the expectations of any of the parties in Judaism at the time. In particular Jesus dealt with the wrongdoing of the people of God not by announcing imminent punishment followed by distant restoration, but by endeavouring to awaken by his words and actions insight into God's present graciousness, and by bearing the consequences of the wrongdoing himself. It was a fulfilment of prophecy which negated a good deal of the tradition of it, just as Jesus fulfilled but also negated other aspects of the Old Testament.[21]

We must consider the bearing of this fulfilment and negation of prophecy on the prophetic task of the church today. Calvin was the one who in the Christian tradition emphasized Christ as prophet, priest and king. He cited in particular Isa. 61.1–2, not the most characteristic picture of a prophet in the Old Testament which, according to the story in Luke 4.16–30, Christ claims to fulfil.[22] However in the New Testament the whole community of Christians is thought of as prophetic,[23] even though within it some would have a particular gift of prophecy within the whole,[24] and were to exercise it for the building up of each one, so that together they would reach their full maturity in Christ.[25]

The early church certainly encouraged the ministry of prophecy. At the beginning of I Cor. 14 St Paul says, 'Make love your aim, and earnestly desire the spiritual gifts, especially that you may prophesy.' The whole chapter is concerned with comparing and contrasting prophesying and speaking with tongues. There are several references to prophecy in lists of the various gifts in the Christian community;[26] and an example in Acts 11. 27–30 of a Christian prophet, Agabus, who came from Jerusalem to Antioch and prophesied that there would be a great famine which, it is said, took place in the days of the Emperor Claudius. In Acts 21.10–12 he also made a symbolic gesture and prophesied the fate of Paul (which was not exactly fulfilled). In I Cor. 14

Paul understands the prophetic ministry as a kind of pastoral preaching, which Paul valued (as against a more showy ecstatic utterance with which the Corinthian church was impressed). Paul says the prophets are to check one another, and make way for one another, very different from the Old Testament attitude. The early church was vigorous and inchoate. Prophets, apostles and teachers are not clearly distinguished from one another. In its earliest years it was also dominated by an expectation of an imminent *parousia* or return of Christ, which gave an interim status to all its activities. This expectation diminished in the course of the first century (though, as I have mentioned, it has never died out), and the Fourth Gospel is free from it. A great theological reconstruction had taken place as the church settled down to an indefinite ongoing existence. The ministry of prophecy diminished. In I Tim. 18, there is a hint that it may be a thing of the past. Already in the *Didache*, a short book which probably dates from early in the second century, and which nearly got accepted into the New Testament, the prophet is viewed with a certain circumspection.[27] He is to be received as one from the Lord, but if he stays for three days or asks for money or anything else for himself, he is a false prophet. Wandering charismatic figures who made self-authenticating claims were a doubtful blessing in churches which were building up a resident ministry. Montanism, which called itself the 'new prophecy' and arose about the middle of the second century in Phrygia and for a time spread rapidly, was a return to an adventist tradition expecting an imminent parousia. In repudiating it the church affirmed the assimilation of prophecy into its general preaching and teaching task. The question then becomes, what should that task be, and whether it is being adequately performed; and in particular whether the church is alert to the ambiguities of religion which it has been a particular contribution of prophecy to stress. The task is part of the whole question of the relation of the gospel of the kingdom of God, and the church as the conscious herald and agent of the kingdom, to the life of the world in which it is placed. To that we must now turn.

3. Prophecy and the church today

The first point to notice is there are now two kingdoms, not one.

The Old Testament prophets addressed themselves to a state which was also a church. In interpreting the signs of the times in the name of Yahweh they regarded the unfolding of human history, as they interpreted it, entirely from the point of view of the vocation, calling, or election of the people of God in their church-state. If the northern kingdom fell to Assyria it was the rod of God's anger against his disobedient people.[28] If Babylon captured the southern kingdom Nebuchadnezzar was the unwitting servant of Yahweh, fulfilling God's judgment on his people although unaware of the fact.[29] If Cyrus of Persia allowed a return from exile of the Jews to Jerusalem he did so as Yahweh's servant.[30] It is not now possible for us as Christians to interpret the tale of human history as if it is entirely concerned, whether for good or ill, with the people of God, although it is often done.[31] For a long time, in pondering on the significance for Christians of the enormous success of atheist Marxism in little more than a century, I interpreted it as God's judgment on a bourgeois form of Christianity, in its failure to rise to the social challenge of the Industrial Revolution, and regarded Marxism as an unwitting servant of Yahweh expressing his judgment on it. But though there may be something in this it is too narrow an interpretation. It puts the church too much in the centre, as if God's gracious purposes for all mankind can only be achieved through the church. This has indeed been a common assumption of Christians. But it presents very great difficulties. Even if one could cope with the salvation of millions of people before Christ by the myth of the descent into Hell, what of the millions since who have lived and died without a knowledge of him, or have only been presented with a distorted picture of him? (I leave aside the question of those who have admired him but could not conscientiously accept him). The church is the self-conscious agent of the kingdom of God, and each Christian has the privilege of a deeper knowledge of God's gracious purposes for mankind than those who are not Christians, but he is working everywhere for the good of the human beings made in his image, and it is the Christian task to discern the signs of his working and to further it. The church is specially related to the kingdom of God; and there is the other kingdom of the structures of life to which it also has to relate. There is a kingdom of re-creation, but also a kingdom of creation. The Christian lives in both at once until the end of time.[32]

The basic moral order belongs to the realm of the human as such, and the ethic that corresponds to it is one in which Christians are bound up in the bundle of humanity in the kingdom of the world. The ethics of the kingdom of God, however, is not directly applicable to life in the kingdom of the world although, as must be emphasized, it is not irrelevant to it. That ethic is summed up in the word love, as translating the Greek word *agape* and the Latin *caritas*. There are many studies of love as Christians understand it. The life and teaching of Jesus and St Paul's picture of love in I Cor. 13 are the chief sources, and I must assume a general grasp of it, and not add to those studies.[33] Notice that we should not talk as if there is no knowledge of *agape* outside the Christian faith. Far from it. For example at least some glimmerings of the unconditional graciousness of *agape* must be known by most parents in their attitude to their children. The Christian gospel builds on this, deepens it, radicalizes it, and universalizes it. Love is shown to be inexhaustible. The more one knows of it the more one finds there is to know. The reward of love is to know more of what it means, the opening of further dimensions of it. Only those of us who have explored it but a little way can talk glibly of it. That is why those whom we think most 'saintly' are most conscious of the gulf in themselves between what they see of the possibilities of love and their realization of it in their own lives. This is not because they have a pathological sense of guilt, but because they have a deeper insight and awareness. Love is inexhaustible. There is always a gulf between what we know *ought* to be the case in our life and what *is* the case. Moral complacency, or boasting (as St Paul would say) is excluded.

If this is the case in our personal lives, how much more is it the case in our collective lives in the kingdom of the world. The possibilities of a group transcending the concerns which give it the necessary cohesiveness to hold together get progressively less the bigger the group becomes, and are least in that comparatively modern entity the nation-state.[34] Yet it is important to stress that there is *some* possibility of group self-transcendence. If there were none group conflicts would never be resolved other than by the stronger suppressing the weaker. Therefore the possibilities of transcendence need exploring and fostering. That must be one of the roles of prophecy, to which I shall shortly return. But it is the relatively lesser range of the possibilities of self-transcendence in collective rather than personal living which lead us to say that the ethic of the kingdom of God does not bear directly on the kingdom of the World. It is as this point that the great questions of the relation of love to justice and to power arise.[35] Christian love cannot avoid the questions of justice as fairness. Even in family life the children in their differences are equally loved by their parents, who nevertheless have to try to be fair as between them, though fairness does not have the last word. Similarly in the kingdoms of this world it is not possible to ignore questions of power, while of course subjecting power to critical scrutiny. There *are* things that belong to Caesar.

These considerations also apply to the church, which is not the kingdom of God but its agent. It might be possible for a small, highly selective group in special circumstances under very strong mutually re-inforcing Christian inspiration to approximate to the extent of self-transcendence which an individual may reach, but it is certainly not the case with the greater church with its land and buildings and paid servants. It faces the same constraints and the same challenges as do other structures in the kingdom of the world. Sometimes it behaves worse than other groups, to the great scandal of the faith; sometimes it ricochets from a rather sentimental attitude compared with the general run, to a more severe one than the general run; and sometimes the resources of renewal on which it can draw (not least the prophetic tradition), lead it rather further on the road to self-transcendence than other groups achieve. At any rate the church has to bring her own behaviour under the test of her own gospel, and resist the temptation to assume that because the gospel she proclaims is of ultimate significance, she herself is exempt from its scrutiny, or that what she may conceive as her interests are necessarily those of the gospel. There is always a temptation to regard the holiness which we ascribe to it, when we call it One, Holy, Catholic and Apostolic, to be too much of a present possession and too little an eschatological challenge and hope.

The task starts with her own life. There is a prophetical critique needed of the pretensions and ambiguities of individual and corporate expressions of the faith. All of us are tempted to over-estimate our own virtue (unless we are afflicted with a pathological self-loathing). All individuals, groups, institutions, nations and churches are subject to the corruptions of pride and power. Religion can mask the face of God. Consequently the church is agent of a gospel which is always searching for personal and collective expression but never fully achieving it. There is an eschatological dissatisfaction built into her faith which means that it can never be at ease in Zion, never satisfied for long with the *status quo*. The kingdom of God relativizes the institutions of the kingdom of the world. In view of this it is disturbing to find how far the church has in practice behaved in the opposite fashion and sanctified the *status quo*. It is true that God is a God of stability as well as change. Indeed without stability change would be anarchic. There are many occasions when we have to say that it appears that any immediate alternative to the present state of affairs, in spite of its blemishes, would be worse in terms of what as Christians we wish to affirm. We rejoice then in the stability of God's created order. But we cannot be prophetic about stability. Nevertheless the fact that stability has been over-emphasized over most of church history does not mean that its importance should be overlooked in the furtherance of radical change. But neither does it mean that the changes going on can be ignored. They need evaluating and either fostering or modifying. That is the work of prophecy, amid the diverse ministries in the Christian church.

In discharging this task how do we find the word of God for today? How is it known? By visions? Ecstasy? Moral judgment? It is known by *discernment*. Visions and ecstasy may be the source of symbolic actions, to which I shall shortly return, but discernment is achieved by putting one's understanding of human life, drawn ultimately from the biblical witness to Jesus Christ, alongside a diagnosis of what is going on today. There is no direct line from a biblical text or passage to a conclusion about the world today. There has to be some evaluation of 'what is going on', which cannot be got from the Bible, but is then brought alongside an understanding of man's life and destiny drawn from the biblical revelation. Discernment involves the ability to grasp the issues of one's own day in a dimension of depth. It involves qualities of character which are deepened by one's faith and worship. From character comes sensitivity, not only to what lies on the surface, but to underlying human reactions and possibilities. It involves hope for the future, based on a faith derived from an understanding of God's actions in the past. But it also involves a judgment on the events of the day, the tendencies at work, and the secondary consequences of possible actions (and not merely the immediate and obvious ones); and this can only come from a knowledge which cannot be drawn from the Bible. It can only come from the experience of living in the modern world and making use of such sources of information as are available. Some of this will come from personal experience; much will depend on others.

This is the more necessary because we cannot assume that God operates directly on the human scene in the way that the Old Testament thought he did. Everything that happened could then be seen as done directly by God. Either his human agents did what he told them; or if they did not, he punished them by what he caused other human agents to do, whether they were aware of his agency or not, or by what he did directly himself. Today, without necessarily being Process theologians, we think of God as 'luring' human agents to fulfil his gracious purposes through their responses to the complex decisions which are continually being made in the web of human life, whether they are aware of God or not. Not everything that happens can be presumed to be directly God's will, still less as being focussed on his chosen people. We have the responsibility of weighing what is happening in the light of criteria drawn from the gospel. The most obvious example is the need in areas of change so rapid as to be called revolutionary, to distinguish what is revolutionary from what is counter-revolutionary.

To exercise this quality of discernment we need information. We need facts. Some of these will come from our own experience and those with whom we chiefly associate; some from the channels of information open to us as citizens, the press, radio and television. Some comes from experts, but in the end we still have to judge the experts.[36] We cannot do without them but they alone cannot settle issues. Medical ethics is an obvious example. Recent developments in biology since the cracking of the genetical code have resulted in issues of medical ethics arising far beyond questions of medical etiquette, and beyond the competence of the medical profession alone to settle, even though they cannot be settled without them.

Facts are necessary. But it is more complicated than that. For facts are seen in a context of significance. 'Bare' facts by themselves do not help. The selection of what among them are worth attending to, and the weightage given to them, are determined by our value judgments. These value judgments come from our overall understanding of human life, that is to say, our philosophy or our religion. So the Christian will find his faith illuminating the facts, as well as forming his character and inspiring his vision in his task of discernment.

At first sight this might seem ominous. Since people have different faiths and philosophies, does it mean that these will lead them to select and evaluate facts differently, so that we shall never get agreement among humankind? Shall we all be shut up with others of our outlook in separate faiths and philosophies without intellectual and moral contact with those of other outlooks? Fortunately not. This brings us back to the element of basic morality in the world, which is shared in some measure by all human beings who are sane enough to be held responsible for their actions. Indeed it can be argued that it is not possible to deny this morality and live consistently. It is at this level that Christians should be seeking allies wherever they can be found. It is no part of their faith to seek to work only with Christians and Christian institutions. Quite the reverse. Encouraging and deepening the understanding of common morality is one of the church's main tasks, without neglecting the furthering of the gospel of the kingdom of God with its radical ethic challenging, probing and pushing further the ethic of the common morality.[37]

Implicit in what I have been saying is the assumption that it is necessary to go beyond the prophets of the Old Testament, and not merely point out in the name of the Lord wrongs that need to be righted, but to suggest steps to remedy them. This is where it is often not possible to say 'Thus says the Lord' so unequivocally. Once we realize that evidence is needed about what is going on, and that this cannot come from the Bible, it becomes clear that there may be more than one way of selecting the evidence and more than one way of interpreting it. There is likely to be a spectrum of judgments on current issues from the clear cut to the very doubtful, about which equally genuine Christians may hold a variety of views. Massacring Jews in gas chambers is at one end of the spectrum; and many of us think that the institution of apartheid in South Africa is nearly as clear cut an issue, if not quite so awful, but obviously most of the Dutch Reformed

Christians there do not agree. At the other end of the spectrum would be details of monetary policy in terms of dealing with inflation, where the evidence is very uncertain. The Old Testament prophets provide dangerous models of black and white denunciation which can hinder Christians from perceiving the ambiguities and ambivalences involved in moral discernment in relation to detailed situations and policies. The inevitable uncertainties at this level mean that the changing details must not be identified too simply with God's word.

The Old Testament prophets appear to us as lonely figures, though of course they had their followers. They are lonely in that their message came to them directly from God. Once we admit that facts are needed to form a judgment, however qualified our understanding of facts, we do not expect to have a direct revelation of these from God. To select and clarify them in many of the complex issues with which we have to deal today – the question of nuclear energy and nuclear weapons for instance – we need inter-disciplinary study, and a group of people to digest the results and present them to us in a way which will help to form our judgments. Church bodies, like Boards of Social Responsibility, can help here; and they can often co-operate with secular bodies, or draw upon their work. The result should be a clarification of the important issues at stake, and of the tendencies at work and the likely consequences of them; an evaluation of these can then suggest lines of action (with arguments for and against), and possibly the recommendation of one of them if a large measure of agreement is arrived at. This last step may not be likely, unless the issue in question turns out to be exceptionally clear cut, but all the previous steps can be exceedingly valuable, even if the last stage cannot be arrived at.

An effort can also be made to reach a halfway house between generalities and details of policy, by arriving at a 'middle axiom'. It is an unfortunate term, but it means roughly a statement indicating agreement, by those from different experiences working together on an issue, about the general direction in which Christian opinion should try to influence change, without going into details of policy on the best way to bring it about. Detailed policies involve many uncertainties on their details and their possible effects, about which opinons are likely to differ among those who are agreed on the general direction to aim for. There are interesting questions concerning middle axioms which are too detailed for this context and I have discussed them in the second Appendix.[38]

The General Secretary of the World Council of Churches, Dr Philip Potter, gave an address at Bad Boll Evangelical Academy in West Germany in May 1981. It was at a Consultation on 'The Prophetic Ministry of the Church'. Towards the end he said: 'Christians and the churches have been enlightened and enriched by researches in the social and economic sciences and in the tough analyses of society which have developed in the last hundred years. We are no longer permitted to indulge in simplistic judgments about ourselves and society.'[39] This is well said. But it indicates that we have moved on this matter a long way from either the Old Testament prophets or those of the early church. We have moved to an age which relativizes what we say in the name of the Lord, since the evidence has enough uncertainty, or even ambiguity, so that the conclusions we draw cannot unequivocally be equated with the Word of the Lord. Moral theology cannot operate in an *a priori* deductive manner on its own; and complete certainty is rarely achievable in questions of practical ethics.

There are efforts to avoid this conclusion. Some theologians of hope cry down this wrestling with what is happening today on the grounds that we are merely dealing with a calculable future based on factors we know already, whereas God is always creating new things and overthrowing the old, and it is this we must herald.[40] There is a truth here, that we must be spiritually ready for the unexpected. But this alone is a most inadequate basis on which to proceed. It gives no guidance whatever on the present. In practice when one asks what such theologians want us to do it turns out to be surprisingly conventional, in spite of all the talk of revolutionary newness. It amounts to what one might call a progressive liberal or radical stance.

The Presbyterian Reformed Church in Cuba in 1977 was more explicit in a statement on its prophetic role when it said: 'The church lives "prophetically" in its members when they become committed participants in the death of the capitalist society and the dehumanizing and decrepit values it represents. Otherwise the church would be converted into a "scandal" for God and a "reproach" for men, and its "destruction will not be long in coming" like that of all false prophets.'[41] This is over-simple.

Indeed, can the church be prophetic? Or has prophecy to be left to individual members, as has recently been argued by Dr Robin Gill, who has maintained that if the church tries to be prophetic it will become partisan and sectarian?[42] There is surely no need to polarize the matter in this fashion. From what I have said there is a whole spectrum of possible positions. The church can operate at the widest global level inter-confessionally, as in the World Council of Churches, or by one confession on its own, or in regional, or national, or local assemblies, synods, councils and conferences, according to the matter in hand. It can promote, or tolerate, special groups for particular purposes (like 'Christian Concern for South Africa' in the UK). It can take up special issues such as slavery, racism, feminism. It can inspire individuals. There is the greatest possible variety. How far agreement can be secured depends on the complexity of the issue, the range of opinion brought into consultation, and the quality of discernment achieved.

Is there any place for symbolic action in prophecy today? Surely there must be room for prophetic gestures. They can be by churches, groups or individuals. Sometimes they strike the imagination and move public opinion when other ways have not done. It is very difficult to judge the right moment, and discernment of a high order may be needed. In the United Kingdom we have had examples of church bodies disinvesting from any enterprise which has significant business in South Africa.[43] A few years ago I was doubtful of the wisdom of this, now I am less doubtful. One thinks of many examples of prophetic gestures, Christian and secular. Did the suffragettes in Britain gain the vote for women more by chaining themselves to the railings of the Houses of Parliament or by their work in the munitions factories of the First World War? Bonhoeffer once urged the churches to abandon all their investments and live on current free will offerings. They showed no sign of doing it; but would it have been wise? What of the Buddhist monks who set themselves alight and immolated themselves as a protest against the Vietnam war? Or Jan Palach in Czechoslovakia who did the same in protest against the invasion of his country by Russia? Did these causes justify the symbolic action? Or what of the Congregational minister and President of the Welsh Nationalist Party who threatened a hunger strike to prevent the Thatcher government from reneging on its election promise to provide an all-Welsh TV channel, when only 20% of the population of Wales speak Welsh?

This last illustration is a reminder that sincerity is no test of rightness. One can be very sincere and make symbolic and sacrificing gestures for very dubious causes. Christians are no exception. I doubt if direct inspiration will do as a justification. I suggest that it is still necessary for the Christian to work through the process of bringing an analysis of what is going on alongside his Christian understanding of life, before deciding that a symbolic action is the best, or a proper, or a desirable way of furthering the cause he wishes to support. The same could apply to corporate action by the church.

We have touched on the need for prophecy to give hope and vision. If the hopes are too unqualified concerning what is possible in history they become utopias.[44] And when the hopes are falsified cynicism, or a reaction to a brutal *real politik*, is likely. On the other hand history is full of open possibilities to human freedom and creativity. There is no limit laid down by God as to what may be achieved if human beings have true visions and are faithful to them. The limits arise out of human flaws; but human beings can be renewed in their inmost spirit and their flaws at least partially overcome. If this is to happen, prophecy needs to accomplish what many think is the reverse of what it is likely to do. It needs to lead to contrition, penitence and renewal. It is easy to wave a big stick of moral discernment against all wrongdoing, especially that of others. Prophecy can lead to this. The corruption of the best is then the worst. But if it does its proper job the resources of prophetic religion will be a source of hope no matter what the setbacks.

4. Prophecy and the life of faith

What is the place of prophecy in the whole conspectus of Christian life and witness? There are four aspects at least on which a brief comment must be made.

(i) Prophecy and contemplation

Sometimes these are opposed as involving activity versus quietism. But this is unnecessary. It is interesting to note that to some extent both are being stressed by the same people.[45] A sense of the relativity of human language which has accompanied the growth in understanding of changing societies, together with the development of specialist sociologies, has led to a relaxation of an attitude which stressed the fixity of liturgical texts. They have been revised, fruitfully on the whole. But the new texts lack the verbal magic of the old and this, combined with a sense of the inadequacies of language in any case to express the deep things of God and his relations with man, have led to the growth of practices of individual and corporate silence. But there has been no suggestion that any lack of concern for the world has been implied in this. It has been rather more a drawing upon the deep well of divine renewal by those fully committed to a sustaining and prophetic task in the world.

(ii) *Prophecy and pastoral care*

These again are often opposed, but there is no necessary contrast between prophecy and the ministry of pastoral care. There is no suggestion that the pastoral ministry is necessarily concerned with helping people to accept and adjust to the *status quo*, though it may be in the short term and in particular instances.[46] The pastoral ministry is much concerned with distinguishing what cannot be changed and must be lived with, from what could and ought to be changed and should be challenged and modified or removed. The pastoral ministry no doubt will 'temper the wind to the shorn lamb', and help those to whom it ministers to learn what is within their particular powers and qualities and what would be too much or inappropriate for them; but it is also especially concerned to help to identify areas of prophetic activity appropriate to their situation, and encourage and fortify them in fulfilling it.

(iii) *Prophecy and the task of reconciliation*

Are prophecy and reconciliation irreconcilable? If the church is not concerned with reconciliation she has indeed abandoned the gospel. Many fear that prophetic activity will mean taking sides in controversial matters and disrupting Christian fellowship. Much could be said about this but I must be brief. It is precisely because of this fear that so many Christian congregations content themselves with harmless generalities which no Christian could disagree with, such as being in favour of peace, without ever relating them to the details of particular issues. By never discussing anything concrete they put themselves on the sidelines of what concerns people most. Once the procedures and limitations I have mentioned for relating the faith to what is going on have been accepted, it is clear that the church ought to be the place where Christians who take contrary attitudes and find themselves in opposing groups can still listen to one another, pray with one another, and learn from one another. Under their auspices it ought to be possible for conflicting groups or their representatives to meet. The more this happens the less a polarization may take place which renders the achieving of a *modus vivendi* between conflicting parties less likely.

When polarization does occur it is impossible not to take sides. In South Africa, for instance, either one supports the cause of the blacks and coloureds and offends the whites, or one supports the whites and offends the blacks and coloureds. There seems no middle ground. And to do nothing overt is tacitly to support the *status quo*, and thus still to take sides. Here is a bitter conflict which looks like getting worse. If Christians find themselves genuinely on opposite sides of it they must take part in the fear of the Lord, but never let go the possibility of reconciliation through the conflict, but not avoiding it. This is a desperate situation, so we must work to avoid polarization if at all possible. But if it occurs the attitude I have mentioned demands great spiritual resources but is not impossible. It was in that spirit that many of my Christian friends fought in the Second World War. They thought it was a Christian duty to stop Hitler (and they had no illusions that if they succeeded a utopia would follow), but they did not hate the Germans in doing so.

(iv) *Prophecy, politics and eschatological reserve*

It must be stressed that the eschatological reserve which lies behind the prophetic critique does not mean an attitude of conservatism which, because it sees flaws in everything existing or proposed, ends in accepting things as they are. This is a criticism often made by the liberation theologians of Latin America of the rest of Christendom. It could mean that. It often has meant that. But there is no necessity that it should. In fact a proper understanding of eschatological reserve means that it should not. That reserve is not an encouragement to quiescence, but a challenge to prophetic activity, a summons to repent and reform unless it can plausibly be shown that at the given moment no better alternative is feasible.

These reflections lead to a further consideration of the economic and political issues which advanced industrial societies present to our understanding of the gospel and the role of the church, and this is the theme of the last chapter. Meanwhile it is clear that prophecy is not incompatible with these other necessary elements in the whole life of the church and, properly understood, is of fundamental and permanent importance within it.

6

Politics, the Church and the Gospel in the Late Twentieth Century

The argument of this book leads from economics to politics. It has attempted to clarify the fundamental economic problems of any society, which are often misunderstood by Christians, not least those in the Christian Socialist tradition, as they are by those in the Marxist tradition of social analysis.[1] I have suggested that the mechanism of the market is the best device for solving these problems over a fairly wide area of economic life, and that there is a good case for the socialist command economies to adopt it.[2] At the same time I have argued that it is vital not to associate the useful device of the free market with an overall philosophy of life, often called that of 'possessive individualism'. Much of the current talk of 'Victorian virtues' is in fact a more vivid way of referring to this. The institution of the market needs to be put into a firm political framework. Left to itself it is cruel and callous. Poverty caused by the cyclical upswing and downturn of the economic system brings disasters to individuals and families which are beyond their powers to guard against or cope with; and these inhuman effects cannot be left to the uncertainties of private benevolence to correct, though the preaching of that virtue which has usually gone with the outlook of possessive individualism assumed that it could. As Berdyaev wrote fifty years ago, 'A person's fate cannot be made to rest solely upon other people's spiritual condition.'[3] It is appropriate to satisfy many through the market process but not basic needs. We should banish from our thoughts any idea that the market is in some sense a 'natural' institution and that any interference with it goes against some kind of human 'norm' and is therefore dubious and needs a special justification. That is to put economic efficiency, in the sense of maximizing the productivity of relatively scarce resources (assuming a basic system of law and order), above every other consideration. And even though many protests against free competition, whether from management or worker, are specious defences of vested interests, the general point remains that efficiency in this sense is only one human desideratum among others. Making decisions between these desiderata is a matter of politics. In short, the market is a human device set up to serve human purposes, to be a servant and not a master. We must not bow down to an idol we ourselves have erected.[4] It is a political decision as to which areas of economic life are to be left to the impersonal verdict of the market and which to be decided by specific public decisions, as it also is to decide the broad parameters of economic guidelines within which the economy has to operate. No government, however devoted to laissez-faire, can escape this responsibility. Issues of economic life inevitably lead to political ones.

1. The necessity of politics

Politics, then, is an inescapable reality. It is no service, therefore, to denigrate politics; nor on the other hand to be starry-eyed about it. Christians are liable to become nervous at this point and to wish to be non-political. This is not possible. To be non-political in the sense of doing nothing is tacitly to support things as they are, and to do so irresponsibly without thinking about it. To be non-political in another sense, that of demanding that all Christians should agree before a political stance is taken, is to assume that the Christian lives in one world or kingdom, not two, with one political policy to be derived from the gospel and applied directly to that world, and in principle able to be arrived at unanimously in the way that the Quakers arrive at the 'sense of the meeting'.

It is too easy to talk of politics as motivated by greed, intrigue, the ruthless pursuit of power and irresponsible self-interest. It is indeed subject to all these corruptions, but it is not geared to them. Voluntary organizations also, at their own level, are subject to the same internal stresses, which can be the occasion of a mixture of scandal and amusement when publicity breaks; and the politics of groups within the church can exhibit most of these traits where it can often be worse because compounded with an air of sanctity, on the grounds that some vital Christian truth is at issue and the honour of God at stake. All these corruptions of politics need exposing and correcting, but it is a failure of nerve to denigrate politics as such.

Similarly the defects of the social capitalist economies, and the growing awareness of the lack lustre character of the socialist command economies, has led recently in some circles to a denigration of the state as centralized, bureaucratic and inflexible, alien and remote from the citizen. That there is evidence to support such complaints is obvious. But we need to be careful. Eternal vigilance against the misuse of state authority, from the tyranny of petty officials upwards, is certainly needed. However the root problem of the modern Western democratic state is not that it has too much power but that electorates give it too little. I have mentioned this before, and dealt with it elsewhere,[5] and must not say too much about it now. In brief, Western societies have produced mass electorates which for the first time have tasted relative affluence, like it, fear that it will be disturbed by change, and do not understand the conditions which make it possible. They demand incompatible policies (encouraged by politicians with short term ends), and are becoming more disillusioned as governments fail to satisfy them. Advanced industrial societies, with their global inter-lockings, are hard to govern, require considerable political sagacity, and policies which need to consider a future longer than the period between elections. National politics therefore needs informed participation and support, not denigration in favour of the small and local. The local is important, but it is one thing to argue for decentralization where possible, and more power and participation at the grassroots, and another to imagine that the major issues can be settled there. It is also sad that the term 'bureaucracy' is almost invariably used in a bad sense. Modern societies need administration which is expert, impersonal and rational. Impersonality can seem regimentation, especially if we have an individualistic view of our rights, and rationality can seem to be a lack of spontaneity, but there has to be a balance struck between the individual and the community in which neither gets all that it ideally might wish. A bus driver who always waited at stops for those who had not quite got to the stop would benefit the individuals concerned, at the expense of all those already in the bus who would be inconvenienced by the increasing lateness of the bus on its journey. Furthermore a healthy society will find scope for all kinds of voluntary organizations, which can be relatively more flexible than statutory ones, but have to watch that they do not go so far as to waste the resources of money and time which has been given them.

In economic matters the state needs to be strong enough to counteract the restrictive interest of cartels, trade associations, professional bodies and trade unions, all of whom have a strong interest in clinging to their present position or in claiming more for themselves by resisting innovation, protecting markets and keeping others out. In a dynamic world this leads to more unemployment. Those who are fearful of the state forget that, however imperfect an instrument it is, since it itself is run by coalitions of interests, it alone is in a position to implement policies which promote solidarity, and needs the back-up of churches and other voluntary bodies in doing so.

However, we must not idealize the state. Experiences of totalitarian states in this century are a sufficient warning of that. Rather let us, with R. H. Tawney, call it a 'serviceable drudge',[6] so long as we realize that it is in our human interest that the state should be strong enough to carry out its necessary tasks. It is not strong states that lead to totalitarianism but weak ones. A strong state is strong enough to have built-in checks against the misuse of its own power.

The Christian gospel is a support in this. The gospel appeal is addressed to persons one by one. A person has a moral centre in a way in which a group has not. But those same persons develop their life, from pregnancy onwards, in structures of life – the family and the economic and political orders – which profoundly affect them long before they are able to take any personal initiative in the matter themselves.[7] The gospel must be concerned with these structures; and that is why in both Old and New Testaments the authorities are taken very seriously, but not absolutely. This concern is not a 'politicization' of the gospel, a term which has been frequently used since it was popularized by Dr E. R. Norman's BBC Reith Lectures in 1978. Politicization means to subsume the gospel under some political programme which, as will be evident, I should deplore; but the accusation is made only if Christians are critical of established institutions; when Christians support them it is accepted without comment and they are not accused of politicization.[8]

Because the Christian faith gives us an understanding of human life and destiny, and because human life is inescapably political, the gospel has considerable implications and resources for the political realm. Every major Christian doctrine bears on it. I will mention all the classical divisions of Christian theology. How they are to be understood and expressed is constantly being re-examined as the Christian community is called to scrutinize its inheritance from the past in the light of its experiences in the present, but these closely related classical divisions of Christian doctrine remain intelligibly distinct.[9] To begin with the doctrine of creation: this stresses the goodness of the created world and suggests that it is a false spirituality which despises it. Men and women as the crown of creation are given a supreme worth as being made in God's image, and this basic equality they have in common is far more significant than the differences between them in sex, physique, intelligence or skills. They are also vice-gerents under God with respect to the rest of creation.[10] Then there is the doctrine of the Fall and Original Sin, whose terminology seems so out of keeping with our understanding of the evolution of human life that we have to express what it stands for without using the term. It stands for the fact that created life as we experience it is not what we think it ought to be. There is a gap between what is the case and what our moral judgment tells us ought to be the case. Human sin is powerful, being most subtle where it corrupts virtues, not when it leads to flagrant wrong-doing. Economic and political systems cannot be built on the assumption that a natural human goodness will flower as soon as the correct social institutions have been constructed. The doctrine of the person of Christ gives further importance to human beings, in the sense that in Christian belief God identified himself with them in a stupendous act of re-creation through the ministry of Jesus, planting the seed of his kingdom in the world as a disclosure of how it ought to run, and a leaven in running it. The Christian social tradition associated with Scott Holland stressed the incarnation as the source of a gospel for society, but it is no more so than the other doctrines. That of the work of Christ, or the atonement, for instance, re-inforces the priority of grace to works, which needs expression in the social order. If the doctrine of creation witnesses to it since, as Jesus said, the conditions of life, sunshine and rain, are given to all irrespective of merit,[11] how much more is the graciousness of God seen in the life and death of Jesus himself. The doctrine of the church concerns the existence of a new community transcending all the barriers human beings erect against one another – personal, economic and political[12] – which is a sign of the pressures God is exerting all the time in all the world, that is to say it is a sign of his kingdom among the kingdoms of the world. Since in this kingdom grace is prior to works, we would expect it to have a strong, communal sense, and to be sensitive to human need rather than personal desert. The doctrine of the sacraments is a further indication of the importance of the created order; very basic products become the assurance of the continued presence of Christ with his church if very simple actions are done with them in a certain context. The tenor of these doctrines is hopeful. They point to the creative possibilities of human life in the world and do not set fixed limits to it. The evil and recalcitrant forces in human life are not as powerful as those of creative renewal through the ministry of Christ. But there are limits, even though not fixed ones. The possibilities are indeterminate, but we are not promised the full realization of the kingdom of God in this life. The last of the doctrines, that of the last things, expresses mythologically the fact that humankind transcends the limits of time and space and is to reach fulfilment in God beyond them. Nothing creative is wasted or lost. This eschatological hope is also the source of eschatological reserve against identifying the gospel with any particular political, social or economic system. As I have previously pointed out that gospel is always in search of political and economic expression, but can never be satisfied for long with its partial achievements. The effect of this is precisely not to say that all political and economic systems are equally distant from the kingdom of God, so that we must make do with whatever we find ourselves living in and cannot hope for improvement. Quite the contrary. The gospel provides us with the concepts in the light of which we evaluate all philosophies, ideologies and religions, as well as the agnosticism which says no overall view is possible for lack of sufficient evidence. In doing so we shall be likely to find overlapping between them and the Christian faith as well as differences. In the political and economic realm it is important to build on this overlap, and a fundamental mistake is to set Christianity against everything else, and to search all the time for actions and insights which are so distinctively Christian that no one else could have come to them.

In all humility we have to recognize that all these Christian doctrines have been perverted in the course of Christian history, or are distorted somewhere today in the varied phenomenon which is Christianity.[13] There have been, for instance, examples of excessive distrust of the created world, including human sexuality; or at the other extreme examples of political Christianity as unpleasant as that of the Ayatollah Khomeini in Islamic Iran today. But corruptions do stand out against a core of tradition. And one ventures to hope that a proper drawing upon the resources of this tradition would introduce a dimension of holiness into politics, the theme of a recent series of Bampton Lectures at Oxford University.[14] Such a dimension would lead to a greater sensitivity to actions and motives, to a deeper discernment in situations, to self-criticism, and a diminished tendency to identify one's judgments too simply with the will of God, and therefore to greater forbearance with opponents whilst still opposing them. It should give a greater stamina if we realize that the Christian life is not an exercise in personal virtue uncontaminated by the constraints of the present and the entail of the mishandlings of the past, but one of responsibility according to one's circumstances; and it should lessen our propensity to sit down under present social injustices because we have got used to them or are not adversely affected ourselves. Politics needs more of this dimension as a better basis for hope, and as a safeguard against fanaticism or despair.

2. *The gospel and advanced industrial societies*

This potential contribution of the Christian gospel to politics has to be made in relation to the quite new civilization which was launched into the world by the process of industrialization, as compared with that in which Christianity was born. How do gospel values relate to it?

(i) *Affluence*

We live in a country of relative affluence. Jesus lived in one of relative poverty. His strictures against trust in riches are clear. He regarded anxiety as a sign of a lack of trust in the continual graciousness of God, and wealth as a main cause of anxiety.[15] How do we move from the New Testament to our world in this matter? Obviously we cannot move with a wooden literalism, but we can try to discern how an insight in one type of society might work out in another.[16] If human life is meant to be a fellowship of giving and receiving under God, trouble arises with the disparity of riches. Greater riches tempt the possessors to make personal provisions for themselves and their families and become as far as possible independent of others. Whatever the standard of life this is the case. If the whole relative standard rises the problem will still arise within it. But that does not necessarily mean the rise itself is to be condemned. In so far as physical and mental drudgery is removed from human beings it is to be welcomed. There is nothing in the gospel which says toil must be preserved for its own sake. There is no reason to reject the washing machine and to stay with the dolly tub, any more than anaesthetics should be rejected and suffering retained for its own sake. Wealth can be misused, whether little or much, by individuals and societies, and there is plenty to scrutinize here without rejecting a growth in affluence.

(ii) *Efficiency*

Is efficiency a virtue alien to the gospel? It is certainly the force behind the economic growth and the resulting relative affluence of the industrialized world. If we are to consider ourselves vicegerents or stewards under God for the rest of creation it would seem that – other things being equal – we should make the most of the relatively scarce resources, and not do less with them than we might. The impetus behind innovation and wealth creation is not an ignoble one, and a wise society must pay heed to it. Wealth creation has been questioned in recent years and there has been a certain amount of propaganda for a 'steady state' economy or even a less affluent one.[17] If its target has been a brashness which often goes with a zeal for wealth creation it is well aimed. But it often goes further, partly because of mistaken inferences from the 'limits to growth' debate,[18] which was discussed in the second chapter, and partly because of the false assumption that there is a fixed amount of trade and economic activity, so that if the relatively wealthy get more wealth, the poor will get poorer. This last belief, although mistaken, is often held because of a very proper concern for the less developed and underprivileged world, a concern which has undoubtedly increased in recent years, though not to an extent sufficient to produce a change of policy by Western governments. In some cases it is not so much a question of huge sums of money needed as of political interest and will. This is a point made in the Annual Report of UNICEF for 1981, where it is stated that 40,000 young children die every day of malnutrition, half of whom could comparatively easily be saved.[19] Apart from this it is largely a question of less restrictive trading policies by the West. We do not make much headway on these because, whilst the general result would benefit everyone, particular groups in the developed countries would be hit and we do not have social mechanisms which help such groups to adapt to unusually drastic economic change. Indeed we leave them to bear a disproportionate burden.[20] Putting our own house in order is necessary if we are to behave in a neighbourly fashion to the less developed countries.

(iii) *Change and unpredictability*

How to cope with change is therefore a fundamental requirement of a dynamic economy. At this moment we are experiencing rapid innovation in information based technologies which will mean that within twenty years or so perhaps only 10% of the labour force will be needed in manufacture and a vast expansion of jobs in service industries, educational, social and leisure will be needed. Moreover, there will undoubtedly be innovations which cannot be foreseen bringing further changes in their wake. We have mentioned the problem of the time span needed to implement policies which depend on developments rationally foreseeable in terms of existing factors. There is, however, a radical unpredictability in human affairs, and it is this that gives point to the theologians of hope who stress the God who is always doing new things and bringing the old to an end. There are several reasons for the unpredictability. One is the element of radical innovation in technological change. If one could conceive of any one such innovation one would be on the way to inventing it. Then, once invented, the repercussions take time to be appreciated, as happened with the smashing of the atom and the cracking of the genetic code (though in this latter case the implications became clear more quickly). There is also a radical fortuitousness in human life, exemplified by the well-known example of the speculation of the historian J. B. Bury concerning the relation of the founding of the Roman Empire to the length of Cleopatra's nose. And while there are statistical regularities in human life, there is also an uncertainty about the future actions of particular persons and the reactions of others to them. So, as Alasdair MacIntyre observes, even if we can identify what 'game' is being played, in order to predict what move you will make, *I* must predict what *you* will predict as to what moves *I* will make . . . and so *ad infinitum*.[21]

(iv) *A Welfare State*

It is because of both predictable and unpredictable change in human affairs that social provisions are needed, not in order to protect people against it, but to prevent its effects being unduly harsh on some. This is where the Welfare State has its place, as the foretaste of a new kind of society made necessary by the continual technological obsolescence of an industrial and post-industrial society. Information technology is a stimulating, and war weapons an alarming, illustration of rapid obsolescence. Gilder says a welfare system should be unattractive, and a bit demeaning, so that the poor will have a spur to get out of it,[22] which is precisely the Victorian attitude we have been trying to get away from since the break up of its Poor Law in the years following the epoch-making Minority Report on it, written by Sydney and Beatrice Webb for the Royal Commission in 1909. Progress was slow, and it was only the experience of the Second World War which led to the invitation to Beveridge to produce his report of 1942 and to the effort after the war to achieve a co-ordinated shape to a Welfare State which would attack the five giants of Want, Disease, Ignorance, Squalor and Idleness so vividly portrayed by him. It proposed a single, comprehensive system of social insurance at subsistence level, based on a flat rate of benefits and contributions (with a small element of National Assistance for exceptional cases), together with family allowances, a comprehensive National Health Service and a full employment policy.

Merely to list these reveals how times have changed. But a

defect was there from the beginning. An insurance rate sufficient for subsistence was not accepted, and the flat rate security benefits never caught up with the rise in earnings or the cost of living. National Assistance which was meant to deal with marginal cases became with its Means Test a pervasive and permanent feature of our society. The Supplementary Benefits Commission which was set up in 1966 to replace it and was dissolved in 1980 had millions of people under its care. Defects of structure can also be demonstrated in the health and educational services. We have, in fact, recreated a version of Disraeli's picture of two nations; those who are dependent on the basic state benefits and those who are able to turn to various occupational schemes. As long as the Gross National Product grew at the rate of about $2\frac{1}{2}\%$ per annum the difficulties were concealed; with the check to this since 1973 they have become increasingly obvious, and the whole conception of the Welfare State is under attack by the radical right. Its fundamental values need re-asserting. Whatever its problems, the alternatives are worse.

This need not be a question of right and left politically. Bismarck after all moved this way in Germany long before we did. And I have already mentioned that the most successful welfare state today is that of conservative Japan.[23] No. There are two different philosophies living uneasily together in Conservatism. One is an organic one, sympathetic to the Welfare State, and the other that of possessive individualism, which is antipathetic to it. It is this which has grown in recent years and succeeded in labelling the other as 'wet'. There is some irony in this, because so many middle-class conservative supporters benefit from alternative and less explicit welfare states, and at the same time do better out of the explicit one because they know better how to operate it.[24]

The root question, however, is not primarily one of slow economic growth or even an absolute fall in productivity, but of what is done with the resources that are available. The evidence seems fairly clear that we are moving into a post-industrial society which, if it handles the transition wisely and does not devote its energies exclusively to propping up the obsolescent, will have a high productivity with a much smaller labour force. On this basis it will move into a service society, paying for the services out of the productivity. Britain is probably experiencing this most sharply because she was the first industrial nation. Routine jobs in which half the working population has hitherto earned a living are disappearing. It is the personal services of this half which will need to be developed and paid for, not the inhumanity of keeping them idle on subsistence benefit. Other changes will be needed, such as a shorter working week and life, and a diminution of the sharp distinction between work and leisure, but these are subsidiary. It is probable that a basic citizen's income should be paid without a means test at a rate about 140% of the higher Supplementary Benefit scale, underpinning other political and industrial policies. However this is not the place to elaborate details of a new economic basis for society to which we need to be moving fairly quickly. The point to note is that the philosophy of possessive individualism is hostile to the whole idea, and bids fair to lead us by an opposite route to disaster.

(v) *Bias to the poor*

In this section we have been considering the new kind of society produced by industry and how the gospel may relate to it. A further point here is that the gospel enjoins a 'bias to the poor'.[25] More accurately we should say that Jesus directed attention to all the disadvantaged, to all those that the majority tended to write off or despise; women, tax collectors, lepers, the poor. He drew upon Old Testament roots in prophetic teaching and the idealistic law of Jubilee (never observed as far as we know),[26] but took it further. God's graciousness is bestowed impartially on all, but at the same time he has a special concern for the disadvantaged.[27] To consider the institutions of society from the angle of those who experience the rough end of them is not something that their more affluent fellow citizens find easy. Only slowly are the poor being heard, only slowly are they acquiring power to affect things and not just to be pushed around. Even the more sensitive service to them in the past has been paternalistic; it has been *for* them rather than *with* them. In the great outburst of philanthropy in Victorian Britain, for instance, we can find few traces of the poor actually themselves having been heard. This is not to idealize the poor, or imply that they are any more far seeing than anyone else; merely to say that without power one is not listened to in the political forum, and a bias towards them is needed to empower them. This is because poverty is not a question of whether one has the bare minimum to exist, but whether one is excluded from the generally accepted way of life of the community and, in particular, whether one is in effect powerless and not able to insist on being listened to.

3. *The challenge of the societies to theology*

I now turn to the challenges to theology itself thrown up by the rapidly changing society of the late twentieth century. In a recent review in *The Modern Churchman* I was quoted as an example of someone who carried on 'iterative theological reflection'.[28] I was surprised to read this, feeling like the man who had spoken prose all his life without knowing it. I now gather that it means accepting a reciprocal relation between theology and other disciplines, in this case the social sciences. This is indeed my position. I think that the effort to 'do good' may be futile, or even harmful, without help from relevant branches of knowledge in understanding 'what is going on' in the world today.

(i) *Ideology and the sociology of knowledge*

One of the most important tasks is for theology to come to terms with the sociology of knowledge and the concept of ideology. The roots of that discipline go back to Karl Marx who taught that ideas are a superstructure of which the base is the relations of production at any given time.[29] Ideas are social products. Also, since the class struggle is central to social change, so the class structure is the key to ideas. Thought is ideological and not, therefore, real knowledge. That is why Marx thought he had discovered a science which does give us real knowledge and thus the key to understanding social change. We do not need to follow the intense discussion of these issues within Marxism, but it is out of them, together with elements of positivistic thought and also American social behaviourism that the sociology of knowledge has come. In Britain the publication of Karl Mannheim's *Ideology and Utopia* in 1936 marked its arrival. Its effect is to relativize accepted truth claims, even its own claims as the sociology of sociology itself is investigated. Theology is not exempt from its scrutiny, and has hardly yet come to terms with it, and needs to. It is only caught out if it forgets or denies that thinking, including theological thinking, arises in a social context, of which it should be critically aware.[30] The question 'In whose interest?' is thought being maintained and developed is always a relevant one; and if we think economic interests are particularly powerful we shall pay particular attention to them. It has been pointed out that at a less fundamental level different types of theology have come from monasteries, from seminaries, or from universities. Their milieu has influenced their characteristics. When, however, we find José Miguel Bonino, the Latin American Methodist theologian, asking 'Who does theology?' and 'Who consumes theology?' and answering 'a limited section of a social class . . . does theology basically for the same community' it is much more serious.[31] He goes on to refer to the need for theology to overcome class captivity, and to uncover the hidden class-bound presuppositions which passes for objective scholarship.

The concept of ideology does raise searching questions about theology as an academic discipline. Not very much, if at all, in an activity like textual criticism, but progressively more as one moves into areas of general human activity. It is not that the truth or otherwise of what is maintained is disposed of by showing the social factors which are associated with it; the question is how far blindness to these factors has affected the content.[32] Indeed changing situations have taught us that 'truth' cannot be totally encapsulated in forms of words, but that the understanding of them is continually reviewed within the community which cherishes them, as the intellectual and cultural situation changes. The sociology of knowledge is a more systematic approach to and extension of this process. At the more homely level of political exchanges we should be more sensitive to the interests to whom the political parties are most alert. Tories to landowners, business management, farmers, shire counties, the military and the police; Labour to skilled and unskilled workers and a section of the intelligentsia (often in public service jobs); and the new Liberal-Social Democratic Alliance to the considerable radical section of middle-class intelligentsia who read the quality papers.

(ii) *The church and the middle class*

It is among these last that the major Christian churches tend to flourish, and who make up the greater part of the membership of its Synods and representative gatherings.[33] So it becomes important what the church does with them. Perhaps the most important is to encourage the spirit of self-criticism, not only personal which is almost always realized at least in theory, but criticism of the social groups to which its members belong. Middle-class people, and paticulrarly the intelligentsia among them, are prone to the illusion that because they are in the middle they are impartial and free from vested interests and ideologies. This is not so. The illusion that one is free from ideology is itself an ideological illusion. It is not that one can be totally free from ideological distortion and think as an embodiment of pure disembodied reason. We cannot escape from our social and cultural skins, but we can become more aware of the conditioning factors in our thought and more able to allow for it. That way lies greater social health. It is right that we should express our interests in the forum of public discussion where other groups express theirs, but dangerous if we are under the illusion that we are completely impartial.

This is of importance when we consider some re-distribution of wealth and income through state policies. This will be largely at the expense of voters in the middle. Of course the most wealthy will suffer but, though their excess of wealth stands out, in the aggregate it is not nearly a big enough proportion of the national wealth to make a significant re-distribution on that basis alone; the middle range of incomes will have to contribute. It is precisely among these that tax revolts are found (and among the highly paid skilled workers who are joining them); and among these that the churches are relatively strong. How can they be persuaded? A greater self-criticism would help them to see the extent to which they want tax cuts on the one hand and social benefits that come from taxes on the other,[34] and the advantages they gain from the other four Welfare States identified by Frank Field.[35] They should also be helped to see that their own well-being depends upon mutual co-operation, and that they themselves need mutual support in meeting the various contingencies that life throws up. Prudential arguments must not be despised. Beyond that Christian people might be expected to see the bias towards equality in the roots of their tradition. As I have mentioned, the general tenor of the Old Testament leaves side by side the idea of justice as impartiality, not favouring one person more than another, and that of a special concern for the poor, and this is not contradicted in the New Testament. How this is related to the empirical inequalities between people is a matter of detailed debate, but it can plausibly be established that there are certain basic human needs which should be secured for each person independent of his ability, potentiality or merit. These include first, the necessities of survival, and second, the space in which to exercise that capacity for moral judgment in life which is distinctive of human beings. Freedom from arbitrary exercise of power over them is one necessity, and so is access to a certain level of health care and education.[36] Poverty is a matter of relative deprivation; and as I have mentioned, it is our job to identify those who are so disadvantaged in society that they are unable to play the part in the community which the majority take for granted, and then devise the means of correcting the injustice.

(iii) *The question of Marxism*

It was a discussion of the sociology of knowledge which led me to these reflections. There are two more matters which theology needs to consider in responding to the new kind of society industrialism has brought into the world. The first is, what judgment is to be made of Marxism? I have already mentioned Marxism more than once. It used to be thought of as a monolithic phenomenon, but now it is clear that it is as pluriform as Christianity itself. In the present context I can but give my own conclusions in a somewhat dogmatic way on a matter of immense fascination and significance. I think it can be shown that Marxism is not the science that it claims to be, a science in the sense that on its basis one can predict the future course of human society. Each of its various theories contains elements of truth, and often elements which were being ignored in the nineteenth century when Marx wrote, but each is sufficiently inadequate as not to provide a sufficient basis for action.

Its economic theories are its weakest and, since it claims these are fundamental, this weakness has had a cramping effect on other Marxist theories in dealing with the dramatic changes in human society since Marx. However since the death of Stalin there has been a flowering of Marxist analysis which would have been better able to cope had it been able to ride more loosely to the economic theories.[37] The trouble is that from a more rigid approach Marxism is a seamless robe so that demoting one element affects the entire fabric. There are systems of Christian doctrine which face the same problem. Nevertheless there has been a good deal of creative Marxist writing recently, some of it so far from the original doctrines as to raise the question as to the limits of what can properly be called Marxist. Again the same situation arises in Christian theology. In a sense we are now all Marxists, in that we can, and ought to, take into account what is of value in Marx's without being Marxists, as we can in Freud without being Freudians. Marx's criticisms of religion will not hold, though they were pertinent to most of the nineteenth-century Christianity he encountered. He was convinced that belief in God reduced the stature of man, whereas Christians believe that God intends the greater autonomy of man within his creation. Marxism in fact gets its moral force from basic categories that are akin to basic biblical ones, and is in a sense a religion dressed up in the form of a science, but a religion which has difficulty in dealing with the category of the personal, and especially with the inevitability of death as it confronts the person. However Marxism is changing as it has to meet any new circumstances, just as Christian theology is changing. The particular form of Marxism embalmed in the USSR is anathema to most Marxists outside Russia. Christian theology must be flexible and wise in approaching Marxism. The time of blank opposition is past. The initiative heralded by John XXIII must be pursued, or rather renewed as far as Europe is concerned, where it came to an end after the Prague 'spring' with the Russian invasion of Czechoslovakia in 1968. In Latin America Christian concern for Marxism flourishes, where the liberation theologians are re-thinking their faith in the light of a Marxist analysis. In the fourth chapter I concluded that while they have no use for its atheism, they allow too much to its claim to be a science.[38]

(iv) *The common good*

The fourth question, raised in a new form by industrial society, is that of the theological concern for the common good. It is a plural society, which is secular in the sense of no longer being subject to church control (as ideally it was in the Christendom situation), and as having varied sources of value judgments in other faiths and philosophies. What is to hold society together? If it is to flourish it must be more than brute force. Indeed the tragedy of the South African situation is that it is hard to see what common ground there is among *all* the inhabitants of that country, and one's fear for its future is precisely that it is only brute force that holds it together for the present.

The problem is to arrive at some consensus on a common morality, which carries a sense of obligatoriness, and also to allow for a range of diversity. However the fact of diversity, which is obvious, and the conviction that (subject to basic public order) each should be allowed to follow his convictions, does not imply that all cultures and communities are equally valid, nor that there is no conceivable way of comparing their merits. The practical problem is to help people to form some common convictions amid the pluralism of society. We have seen that capitalism pre-supposes virtues which it does nothing to foster, and may indeed undermine. Sociologists are stressing that society depends on civic virtues and asking where are sources of them today? Bryan Wilson, for instance, says that the rationality and impersonalism of modern society produces a dessicated hedonism of the market, whereas society depends on a sense of commitment, obligation, responsibility and disinterested good will.[39] The present economic situation nicely illustrates the point. It is to the general interest to agree on a policy of wage restraint and the closure of inefficient factories, but in the short term each group gains if others restrain while it wins an extra large pay rise or a government subsidy. Again, if permanent inflation is expected it is discounted in advance in making wage and salary claims, and those groups with extra industrial muscle can win a temporary advantage before the rest catch up. So a perpetual pay, benefits and subsidy scramble develops, and the more participation in decision making grows the more it is accentuated.[40] How can this be corrected? Partly by better institutions, since the free market by itself is not acceptable (and we have abandoned a promising initiative like the Prices and Incomes Board); but also by a greater devotion to the common good as compared with sectoral interests.

Is this a pipe dream? Theologians are divided on this. The Catholic tradition stresses the concept of the common good. Some Protestant theologians are suspicious. André Dumas, for instance, argues that it tends to pre-suppose a metaphysics of harmony, a stable society, and is advocated by those with a favourable position in society, since it offers a justification for the privileges of conservatives.[41] Such a conception of it had never occurred to me! I have associated the common good more with basic human needs, with the basic conceptions of practical reasonableness in morality, and with a view of society as made up of groups with conflicting interests which have to be held within some conception of a common good. The moral philosopher, Alasdair MacIntyre, is dismissive of any appeal to the common good or the common moral traditions of promise keeping, truth telling and benevolence because he thinks that moral pluralism has become too great. Rational analysis of moral decisions with its stress on universalizability has failed to show that it cannot be flouted without inconsistency (it cannot deal with the fanatic); whilst existentialist thinkers stress personal choices which can be infinitely varied and not subject to rational discussion. He maintains that the list of basic virtues is irreconcilably diverse; for example humility, thrift and conscientiousness could not appear in any list of Greek virtues. It is hard to establish any basis for the common good, or to get beyond the contention that it is to our long term advantage that people *in general* should be just. But why should *I* be, if I can get away with it?[42] Our society cannot hope to achieve a moral consensus.

It is not possible to consider this position in detail. It is the direct opposite of the moral tradition, recently and powerfully re-stated by John Finnis, that there are certain forms of human good which are self-evident, and that the impartial pursuit of them is implicit in human nature; he cites life, knowledge, play, friendship, aesthetic experience, use of the reason, and religion. I think MacIntyre is too negative. He is right to deny that there is a necessary unity and harmony of virtues and to affirm the possibility of tragic conflicts between them. But because of his attack on liberal democracy he does not give enough attention to the public virtues of tolerance and justice, and the moral practices needed for a sustainable plural society. It is true that it is impossible to prove that one should follow a basic morality to someone who denies it; one can only give a moral reason for doing so. It is also difficult, even though logically possible, to live consistently by denying it. And although it is also true that lists of basic moral virtues vary, they do not do so to a radical extent. One could adapt a concept of Wittgenstein and say that there is a 'family resemblance' between them, though no one society holds to all of them.[43] The similarity of the Tao in different faiths and philosophies remains striking. Christian theologians need to affirm and foster it. It is needed as a basis for political life, whilst the gospel points to a further dimension which illuminates and challenges it. Within this affirmation social conflicts must not be evaded. They must be exposed, lived through and a tolerable resolution sought. The church should be able to carry the inevitable tensions within its membership that this will involve. Too frequently it avoids engagement for fear of spoiling the fellowship.

4. The role of the church in society

What should be the role of the church in relation to the society we have been discussing? I take it for granted that the church is primarily engaged in building up a worshipping community whose members will corporately and permanently bear witness to the gospel faith and ethics. It is alarming that many of the most significant moral developments in this century have begun largely outside the churches; the emancipation of women is an example. Bearing witness to gospel ethics leads to a social theology and to politics. In my view the first political task of the church is to strengthen the sense of a common morality in the community, the moral virtues or basic human decencies which Adam Smith pre-supposed. To my mind this is fundamental, but it is rare to find it realized. Verbally the church talks of evangelism, and practically it is pre-occupied with maintaining traditional structures in a time of inflation, so that it overlooks the fact that the strengthening of the concern for the common good, and structures that promote it, is basic to a plural society. In a sense this is a re-call to a traditional 'legitimizing' role of the church but at a much deeper level than merely supporting the *status quo*, which is aware of the gulf between basic moral concepts and the expression of them in existing institutions.

Within the church some who are most pessimistic about society advocate the creation of Christian groups which either temporarily withdraw from or are content to make only a local impact upon the wider society. Similarly MacIntyre is true to his pessimism that there is no hope of achieving a moral consensus in our society, and that 'modern politics is civil war carried on by other means'. He cannot see any tolerable set of political and economic structures which can be brought in to replace the structures of advanced capitalism, and calls for new forms of local community to sustain intellectual and moral life in the new dark ages already upon us. The barbarians now are within. We need another St Benedict.[44] Alistair Kee takes much the same line at the end of *Seeds of Liberation*.[45] Peter Berger suggests the churches should develop islands of authentic humanity in large technocratic societies, where people can know one another. I have heard it said that the churches should take advantage of the retreat into the private in dissatisfaction from bureaucratic and alienated work situations, and that they should focus on the fragility of human institutions, and foster ritual and communal action within the congregations. I think this is wrong advice. Islands of authentic humanity are indeed necessary, but only so long as they do not become islands of contentment but promote social responsibility. This is the strong point of the basic communities in the church in Latin America; they do both. The church must articulate the whole of experience, not a fragment of a fragment of life.

What is the place of symbolic actions? There is always a place for these, so long as they are not made the basis of an entire Christian political strategy.[46] Acted parables and prophetic signs often speak louder than words. Mother Theresa's work among the poverty-stricken and dying in Calcutta is an obvious example. Dr J. J. Vincent has recently written of his Urban Theology Unit in industrial Sheffield, which sets out to be a British example of identification with the poor.[47] He rightly points out that the structures of the church may suit middle-class areas, but they do not fit the inner city, and that the suburban churches are mostly indifferent to the inner city. He wants to re-enact the story of Jesus in the inner city according to criteria from St Mark's Gospel, and calls middle-class people to identify with the poor by living a community life among them and staying there. It is indeed a deeply Christian vocation for some to commit themselves to this alternative local life-style. But there are wider considerations which need to be raised. Dr Vincent criticizes community workers for making people dependent upon them, a danger of which they are well aware, but one to which the middle-class people who settle in working-class areas are equally prone. I am sure Dr Vincent would agree, though he does not say so. However, it his wider perspective that raises queries. He does not make clear that in many inner city areas members of ethnic minorities settle for a while and then the more enterprising move. Those remaining, often the poor white families, are less enterprising and part of the 'submerged tenth'. Identification with them is a Christian necessity, but it is fanciful to say with Dr Vincent, that the seeds of revolution in Britain lie with them, and that 'the beginning of a new humanity may yet emerge among precisely those for whom the wonders of the technological age are forever closed'.[48] Moreover, he universalizes his symbolic action in an illegitimate way. Christianity, he says, must be sectarian.[49] There is a direct line from St Mark to his community, which is equivalent to the kingdom of God in Pitsmoor. It is an alternative Christ-centred way of doing politics, native to Christianity itself.[50] Human systems will not work.[51] It is these large claims which are unfortunate. The gospel cannot so simply be identified with his community or his view of politics. Poverty cannot be tackled solely in an inner city context, nor even only at the level of local government. It involves national policies. Both local community witness and wider political initiatives are needed, neither polarized against the other.

So what can the 'great church' do with respect to the economic and political task? In discussing this I am well aware that the most significant impact of the church in the political, economic, social and industrial field will be through her members as citizens and in their jobs, and the organizations associated with both. This is a point made decisively by J. H. Oldham in his section of the book sent to all members of the 1937 Oxford Conference on 'Church, Community and State' shortly before it took place.[52] But it is not my concern to develop that aspect now. I am concerned with the corporate activity of the great church as a significant social institution, as a source of the formation of the powers of discernment of her members. By the great church I mean all the major Christian confessional traditions, who all accept in some way or other a responsibility for society. Whether they are established churches (as is the case in England and Scotland) is not a very significant matter, unless it misleads those churches to imagine that because the outward structure of a Christendom situation remains the inward reality is still there. Its demise means that the churches have to consider how to influence without controlling, however indirectly or subtly, social institutions.

'Critical solidarity', a phrase coined by the former Secretary of the Church of England's Board for Social Responsibility,[53] is a good one to express the relation of the church to political authorities, provided both words are given equal weight. Solidarity is necessary because the task of government is so difficult, whether central or local, in producing some tolerable realization of the common good amid so many conflicting interests. But critical solidarity is needed because the church's task is more than to provide a sacred canopy overarching the social order.[54] The radical prophetic element in the Judaeo-Christian tradition, and the eschatological reserve which follows from it, should prevent an uncritical solidarity with the authorities, though it has not done so in the history of Europe to anything like the extent it should have done. The easiest way for the churches to be popular in recent centuries has been, and still is, for them to be nationalistic. Within that nationalism the strong identification in the nineteenth and early twentieth centuries of the Church of England with Toryism and the Free Churches with Liberalism was a melancholy aberration. Accepting an overall responsibility for public affairs, the church needs to be self-critical about her own structures and economic interests, and about which persons and groups she most easily identifies with and listens to, and the effects of these factors on her judgments. A picture of herself as impartially giving warnings and encouragements to all from a disengaged position herself is too simple to be convincing.[55] Responsibility involves being involved in complications, differences of opinions, and possibilities of misjudgment.[56] They have to be lived with. The exercise of the capacity for discernment and of reconciliation in the midst of conflicts is a never ending task.

Who are the heirs of Tawney and Temple? It is well to end these reflections by returning to where they started: the legacy of the Christian socialist and social tradition in this country since it came to life again with the Christian Socialist movement of F. D. Maurice and his friends. The question was raised in connection with Tawney by Raphael Samuel of Ruskin College, Oxford, in two articles in *The Guardian* in 1982 criticizing the appropriation of Tawney by the new Social Democratic Party.[57] He criticizes the SDP for thinking of politics in temporal and not spiritual terms, and as a pursuit of the arts of government rather than a struggle between darkness and light. He says it lacks a sense of the

numinous; it eliminates the religious language in English socialism as handed on by Tawney, who saw the market as a seat of
corruption as against a system of workers' co-operation and self-
management. To this Michael Young replied, truly enough, that
Tawney belonged to the libertarian as well as the egalitarian
tradition in socialism, but he did not deal with the wider issues
raised by Samuel. There is some truth in what Samuel says, in
that false political philosophies need exposing, and I have made
clear my criticism of the philosophy of 'possessive individualism'.
But the important point is to separate political and economic
policies, as they change from century to century, from these over-
all philosophies, and to regard detailed policies with an eschatological reserve.

However, whilst never forgetting liberty, Tawney particularly
emphasized equality for the sake of fraternity. And it is equality
which has been the moral force behind the socialist movement,
and not the question of ownership. There are various forms of
ownership, centralized state corporations, autonomous state
corporations, various forms of co-operative enterprise, private
companies and one man freelance businesses. There is a place for
all, and none is a panacea. Nationalization of itself does not solve
problems of restrictive practices, unreasonable wage demands or
government ordered price rises as a form of covert taxation. Over
most of Western Europe the state sector has in fact been promoted more by governments of the right. The Nazis controlled
everything and owned little.

Equality is one very important primary criterion by which to
evaluate policies designed to deal with the basic economic problems which any society has to solve. In addition to those which
have already been mentioned there is the balance between consumption and investment, which involves a balance between
present and future generations, and which will need to be an
over-all political decision whatever the forms of ownership. In
dealing with such problems we have seen why it is important to
make use of the market mechanism where it can be useful. For
instance, if labour is not to be directed there must be some incomes policy with differentials to attract it or to retain it as the
case may be. The question is, how great shall the differentials be?
Christians do well to regard the present distribution of income,
and still more of wealth, as offensively unequal, besides being

increasingly unsuitable to a society where the limits of the power of the appeal to personal consumption are beginning to be seen.[58]

The heirs of Tawney and Temple will live within the ambiguities both of the Christian religion as institutionally expressed or individually lived, and with the ambiguities of economics and politics. The Christian is sustained by a gospel which searches these ambiguities with a powerful searchlight at the same time as it provides the resources of renewal, hope and encouragement for living with them. The Christian does not lose his vision or his staying power in grappling with the nitty gritty of political and economic life, and he keeps before him as the proper aims for the social life of human persons, not so much the individualistic virtues of standing on one's own feet as independently as possible of others, but the virtues of solidarity and community. Imperfect as it is, life in the church is clearly meant to express this. The New Testament could hardly be more explicit about it, and in attempting it the church is meant to point towards a mutuality which God's graciousness wills for the wider social structures of mankind. A church which attempts this needs the assurance to be flexible in her structures, in her priorities and in her willingness to work with the many different levels of commitment which is found among her membership in a plural and post-Christian society. Profound conviction at the centre and an indefinite boundary at the periphery might be thought a sociological monstrosity, combining the features of sect and church.[59] But it is not impossible. Indeed it is a truly catholic position, and one which if he were writing now, I think Scott Holland would endorse.

He lived at the end of the pre-ecumenical era. Our century has seen a tremendous struggle towards unity and renewal in the churches. We call it the ecumenical movement. It was largely born out of shame at the weak witness of a divided church which participated in launching a world war from Europe, the heartland of Christendom, and was later to launch a second one. A more adequate political and economic witness is part of the search for renewal. A Christian is driven to believe that a renewed church is of immense importance for humanity, for it will have to engage creatively with those of other faiths and ideologies. Our theme of church and society in the late twentieth century is of key importance. Yet, as Richard Dickinson says in a survey of the work of the World Council of Churches with special reference to the Commission on the Churches' Participation in Development, we need a realistic view of the church.

> How shall we come to a modest and accurate view of the churches – neither too grandiose, powerful and prophetic, as if the churches were always on the side of the righteous and always struggling for justice, nor abject, viewing the churches as unfaithful, always in collusion with the *status quo*, always spiritualizing and other wordly, always being unprophetic?[60]

The more the church is aware of her ambiguous witness the more she will be able to tackle the internal obstructions which slow the road to unity and renewal and constrict her ability to cope with the economic and political tasks of our time.

Appendix 1: A Note on the Social Theology of Radical Christian Communities

We should note the persistence in the Christian tradition of communities of protest against all the main currents of contemporary opinion and practice. These communities are often called 'sectarian'.[1] Some have been based on a pietism of withdrawal from the evils of society, but by no means all saw themselves in that light. Rather they saw themselves as making an organized protest by establishing alternative forms of community life which should be a pointer to what ought to be thought normal for all. Inspiration has come from the powerless position of the early Christians in the Roman Empire, and behind that from Jesus and his disciples in the gospels. However, the discipline of these communities has not usually been made necessary by restrictions imposed by the external civic situation, but by the internal obedience of the community to the gospels as they understood them. The aim has been to give positive expression to a communal counter-culture without denying concern for those involved in the dominant culture, whilst not accepting responsibility for managing it for fear of complicity with evil. 'Whilst we have time let us do good unto all men, especially to those of the household of faith' (Gal. 6.10) does not imply an exclusive concern for those of that household. Characteristics are an absence of coercion, the surrender of property, and sharing. There is a long history of such communities from Reformation times and before. One thinks for instance of 'Christ's paupers' in the Middle Ages, Gerard Winstanley and the Diggers[2] on St George's Hill in Surrey in the Commonwealth period, and of Mennonites and Hutterians, and various communities within and outside the mainstream churches today.

Leaving aside monasticism, which depends on the outside world to replenish its personnel, these other Christian alternative communities have been very varied, though sharing this common New Testament inspiration. I think there is always a place for radical positions to be taken by individuals and communities which call into question all current assumptions, and I am quite sure some Christians are called to such a witness, and that other Christians should recognize this and be alert to what they say and do. The vocation to be a pacifist on Christian principle is the most common example of this witness. Such individuals and communities are sometimes in a position by virtue of it to take initiatives which are not seen by the rest of us and may, indeed, not be possible for us. On occasion this is of central importance. For the most part, however, their witness can only be marginal to the problems of the political order, which are the concerns of this book. However I do not want to be dismissive in fact whilst on the surface paying compliments to them. Initiatives have to start somewhere. Sometimes they gather momentum and modify the behaviour of the great society, and not only the communities of protest. We need to be alert to this possibility. There is always an eschatological question mark against any political and economic order. We should not neglect any possible source of correction, even though we have the responsibility of sifting what is suggested by an ethic of perfection in terms of the obligations which an ethic of responsibility, also inspired by the gospel, imposes upon us in the great society.

Those of which I am speaking cannot be dismissed as Manichean (like the Cathari, for instance). Nor, as I have said, are they adopting a pietistic withdrawal from the world. Those who do that are usually either comfortably placed, and their a-political attitude is basically spurious, or are so deprived that they seize on religious consolations in default of any other. Rather these radical Christian communities claim to be expressing a socially responsible and, they would claim, in the last resort *the* socially responsible, Christian social faith and life. This is where I part company. In my view, as an eschatological sign of a kingdom of God already in being, but struggling to be more fully realized, they have their place in the rich variety of Christian witness. Usually, however, they want to claim more, and to be seen as realized or proleptic examples of a social order which does not, but ought to, exist. I think it could not exist, and that therefore the main responsibility rests with the great majority of Christians who have to wrestle with responsibilities in the plural world in which they are placed, permanently living in two kingdoms not one. That is why I think they are marginal to the theme of this book, though not to be ignored.

Appendix 2: Middle Axioms in Christian Social Ethics

It has been held that there is a middle ground in questions of social ethics, between general statements and detailed policies, which it is appropriate for the church to occupy. This raises the question of the unfortunately termed middle axioms which played a considerable part in ecumenical social ethics a generation ago, but have not figured much lately. In 1971 I wrote a short article on them for the journal *Crucible*.[1] Since it became rather inaccessible I included it in *Explorations in Theology 9*, 1981; and it has been criticized by Professor Duncan Forrester of Edinburgh University in his chapter in *Christians and the Future of Social Democracy*, 1982. Discussion of the term by others never quite died out, but references have tended to be dismissive and in passing. An example is a recent ecumenical report on political ethics which says: 'Rather than developing a blue print for an ideal political order or defining "middle axioms" for an ecumenical political ethic, the consultation considered witness and solidarity as the areas needing priority attention in the further process.'[2] This is a mistaken alternative, because if the effort to arrive at middle axioms is justified, their aim is to be a stage in clarifying what should be done in implementing whatever general goals the Christian church may wish to forward, whether they are those of witness or solidarity or some other ones.

In my judgment middle axioms are frequently misunderstood. The issues involving them need restating in terms of the problem they attempt to deal with, their nature, the means by which they are arrived at, their possibilities and limits, and the alternatives to them. This judgment was reinforced by a paper which appeared in *The Annual for the Society of Christian Ethics 1981*, by Dennis McCann, on which I shall draw.[3]

I

The problem which middle axioms address is easy to state. If it be granted that the Christian faith should shed light on contemporary public questions of moral decision, and that guidance might well be expected on these matters from the churches, how should they set about giving it, and how detailed should it be? The wide variety of opinions on them among Christians is evident. The most common tactic, certainly in Protestant circles, is to stick to basic agreed moral generalities or principles, which cannot be disputed because they have no specific content. Preachers often do this, and so do church statements. At one time I made a collection of examples of both. I give one example. Some years ago I heard an eloquent sermon concerning a woman whose husband was killed in the First World War and her son in the Second. The question was posed, how can a Third World War be prevented? The answer given was a more sustained proclamation of the gospel. No doubt the preacher felt some assurance that he had himself proclaimed the word of God, but his contribution in terms of the problem he posed was utterly vacuous. It was like the 'if only' type of remark, which says that 'if only' people or groups would not behave in the way they do, and especially if they behaved as Christians ought to, the problem would be solved, or there would not be one in the first place. Again, often when Christians divide into groups at a meeting to discuss a particular moral issue, reports are brought back that there was a useful discussion, but 'of course' no conclusions were reached. There the matter is left. Some discussion is certainly better than none, but is it satisfactory if it is not possible to do more than give a general airing to different views?

On the other hand if detailed recommendations are put forward there is a widespread and understandable belief that the issues are too involved and the details too uncertain to warrant such a prescribed conclusion. If it is done in the course of a sermon people are apt to say 'I don't like politics in the pulpit', and although this often means 'I don't like politics which I disagree with in the pulpit' the objector has a point. There are better places for utterances of this kind. The church of England's 1982 report on nuclear warfare is an illustration of another facet of the problem.[4] It was appointed by the Board for Social Responsibility and made up of only six members and a secretary. It produced twenty-two recommendations, three of which were concerned with the phased unilateral abandonment by Britain of nuclear weapons. Since it was clear to the members themselves that more than one policy would be drawn from the evidence they analysed, and since part of their argument depended on an estimate of the possible consequences of possible actions, it was not surprising that a majority of the General Synod when it came to debate the report took a different line. The exercise was without doubt a useful one. Whether it would have been better if the report had stayed at the level of middle axioms I shall consider later.

There are ways round this problem. One is to evade it by denying that Christianity has anything direct and specific to say on issues of social ethics. This is in practice the attitude of many churchgoers. They listen in the scripture readings to the radical challenge of the gospel and say to themselves in effect, 'We must be realistic and practical people. We know the world does not live like that and we have to live in the world as it is. It would be nice if gospel ideals were acted on, but they are not.' An opposite way is to assume on certain issues that a clear and detailed Christian directive can be arrived at on the basis of a biblical text or texts, or from the alleged self-evident deliverances of Natural Law, buttressed if necessary by the teaching authority of the church. In practice this method is almost confined to sexual issues such as divorce, contraception or homosexuality but, apart from the difficulties each of these raises, there are vast areas of moral decision in economic, social, industrial and political life which have still to be faced. I mention all these areas not because this is the place to discuss them, but to indicate the general background against which the question of middle axioms is set.

II

It was first formulated in 1937 at the Oxford Conference on 'Church, Community and State'. The crucial passage occurs in the preparatory volume,[5] in the section of the book by Dr J. H. Oldham.

> The Gospel is not a code of morals or a new law. But the new mind which is formed in those who have responded to the revelation of a new reality in Christ must express itself in new forms of behaviour. It belongs to the prophetic and teaching office of the church to expound the implications of the Christian understanding of life and to make clear the kind of behaviour to which belief in the Gospel prompts.
>
> Such broad assertions as that Christians are bound to obey the law of love or strive for social justice do not go far towards helping the individual to know what he ought to do in particular cases. On the other hand, there is no way by which he can be relieved of the responsibility of decisions in concrete situations. To give him precise instructions to be literally carried out is to rob him of his moral responsibility as a person. It is not the function of the clergy to tell the laity how to act in public affairs, but to confront them with the Christian demand and to encourage them to discover its application for themselves. Hence between purely general statements of the ethical demands of the gospel and the decisions that have to be made in concrete situations there is need for what may be described as middle axioms. It is these that give relevance and point to the Christian ethic. They are attempts to define the directions in which, in a particular state of society, Christian faith must express itself. They are not binding for all time, but are provisional definitions of the type of behaviour required of Christians at a given period in given circumstances.[6]

To some extent similar thoughts were expressed in the Pastoral Constitution of Vatican II, where in talking of the task of the laymen as citizens in the world it says: 'Let the layman not imagine that his pastors are always such experts that to every problem which arises, however complicated, they can readily give him a concrete solution, or even that such is their mission.'[7]

Oldham went on to urge that this field of common study anp thought was where ecumenical co-operation was most needed and likely to be most fruitful. It would help the churches to see their proper tasks more plainly among the confused struggles shaping the contemporary world, not least because it would call on the best Christian minds and deepest Christian insights from the wealth of traditions within the universal church.

William Temple referred to middle axioms in his introduction to the Malvern Conference volume of 1941.[8] It was also taken up in a report to the General Assembly of the Church of Scotland in 1942.[9] But the first substantive treatment after Oldham of the concept was in 1946 by John Bennett in *Christian Ethics and Social Policy*.[10] He discusses them by giving examples (for instance that Christians should give critical but definite support to the United Nations), and by contrasting the method of using middle axioms with four other Christian social strategies: the traditional Catholic, the sectarian Pietist, the identification of Christianity with particular social programmes, and the double standard type of separation between personal and public life. Bennett makes clearer than Oldham that middle axioms involve both the relevance of the Christian faith to public issues and also its transcendence over any particular policies for dealing with them; and also that an element of empirical judgment on the current situation is involved, not merely in arriving at detailed policies, but also at the level of middle axioms, so that questions of the autonomy and competence of different intellectual disciplines arise.

Two years later Reinhold Niebuhr, writing in a book arising out of the first Assembly of the World Council of Churches at Amsterdam, said in a footnote:

> The Oxford Conference sought a middle ground between a Christian view which offered no general directives to the Christian with regard to social and political institutions, and the view which tried to identify the mind of Christ too simply with specific economic and social and political programmes. For the ecumenical movement, in the opinion of many, this middle ground is still the proper basis of approach.[11]

Greater clarification was needed and, in default of it, misunderstandings began to arise. Paul Ramsey's *Basic Christian Ethics* is an early instance of this.[12] He was not opposed to the concept, and granted that there are stages of particularity between (1) axiomatic first principles of moral reasoning, (2) general and provisional but non-axiomatic directions for social practice, and (3) concrete proposals for immediate adoption by legislation or other means. But, he asked, what holds these three together? 'What stands between a "universal ethical principle" and a "middle axiom" or between one of these and specific plans for action? Surely not another "middle axiom"?'[13] To raise this question is to treat middle axioms as if they are a middle term in a process of deduction between principle and situation. Paul Lehmann makes the same assumption when he criticizes them because 'there is no way in logic of closing the gap between the abstract and the concrete'.[14] It is part of his argument for a *koinoinia* ethic, involving a direct perception of what God at any particular time is doing in the world to make and keep human life human. This is known as contextual ethics. It is not my concern now, and as an alternative method for arriving at detailed conclusions it has enormous, indeed fatal, difficulties.

An article by Ralph Potter Junior in 1972 criticized middle axioms,[15] and this is the starting point of the one by McCann. Potter pre-supposes a prescriptive view of ethical language, as disclosing the logical entailment between general moral principles and particular imperative conclusions. The structure is:

Inference from universal imperative sentences
Indicative minor premiss
Singular imperative conclusion[16]

McCann suggests an example of this procedure which might be constructed on the basis of Gutierrez' liberation theology:[17]

Love one another as I have loved you[18]
To make a socialist revolution is to love one another today
Make a socialist revolution.

This is unconvincing in itself, since the middle term which is merely repeated in the conclusion is not clear enough in view of the many possible meanings of a 'socialist revolution'. The middle axiom 'to make a socialist revolution is to love one another today' is possible only if it were more specifically unpacked and cogently supported by evidence; but this would involve analytical and evaluative techniques in considering evidence, unsuitable for such a logical procedure. Such a procedure involves a mistaken understanding of the term, for which the word 'axiom' is responsible. It has been interpreted in terms of logic when it was meant to be no more closely related to logic than either term in Natural Law is to physical nature or legal statutes.

Middle axioms cannot be forced into the structure of ethical prescriptivism. Moral theologians must indeed take account of the work of moral philosophers, and cannot remain remote from the arguments that range around prescriptivism, but they have no cause to rush to its defence. Moral reasoning and logic are not identical; the former is much more piecemeal and open-ended. Ethics is not a precise discipline. Absolute certainty in it is rare. As Christians we follow an 'ethical pilgrimage with patience and perseverance, sustained by faith hope and love.

James Gustafson refers to middle axioms as 'anchors and compasses' for Christian ethics.[19] Referring to this, McCann says:

Anchors and compasses, of course, are required for successful navigation. Compasses help those at sea to get their bearings and anchors help to minimise drift in troubled waters. It would seem that no less than sailors in a ship socially active Christians need 'anchors and compasses'. Since on this view the Church is less like a lighthouse on the coast and more like a ship at sea, a skilful reading of whatever signs are available is required to keep a steady course. Middle Axioms, in other words, provide such a reading by integrating the disparate elements of 'conceptual populations'[20] launched under the flag of Christian social ethics and giving them a coherent sense of direction. As J. H. Oldham and others insisted they are meant to discern the signs of the times. No more and no less.[21]

They can be arrived at only by inter-disciplinary work between theology, moral philosophy and various disciplines relevant to the area under investigation, and also by drawing upon relevant practical experience from among those involved in it. I agree with McCann when he says that the formulating of middle axioms is the central task of practical theology, whether Protestant, Anglican or Catholic if it is to be coherent in understanding the historic situation of modern Christianity and its practical implications. But I think it unfortunate that in his book he calls two concepts of Reinhold Niebuhr middle axioms: these are 'the tests of tolerance' with respect to ideological conflicts, and 'the balance of power' with respect to political organization.[22] These are more like Paul Ramsey's 'action and decision orientated principles' in that they do not get as far as a judgment on a particular situation. Both of Niebuhr's concepts can be arrived at by reflecting on the implications of the Christian faith for the human situation in any age. They are a stage towards middle axioms in that they involve some reflection on human societies whereby it is realized that conflicts of outlook and rival power centres are perennial features of human life. Middle axioms, however, are not concerned with universal situations but with current ones; and in a descending order of particularity from global to national, regional and local situations. This means that they combine insights derived from the Christian faith with some analysis of 'what is going on' today which involves empirical investigation and judgment on the significant trends, and on the direction in which policies should move.

C.-H. Grenholm makes the same mistake as McCann when he says that the concept 'the responsible society' is a middle axiom.[23] The concepts at the heart of it could be used for evaluating any social order. They were worked out in this century but are not specially related to it. The same applies to its successor in ecumenical social ethics, 'the just, participatory and sustainable society'.

III

The formation of middle axioms begins from reflecting on what is implicit in the gospel as it bears on human life, and the way human beings ought to behave towards one another in the social order to do justice to the humanity of each. An understanding of *agape* is fundamental, but within it there are various concepts none of which can be pursued without reference to the others. The French Revolution's liberty, equality and fraternity is one example. (It should be noted that the secular associations of this triad illustrates an important point, that these derivative 'principles' from the gospel, as they are sometimes called, are not peculiar to it. Others, as well as Christians, can stand for them. This is fortunate. Allies are needed.) William Temple referred to freedom, social fellowship and service as derivative principles.[24] R. H. Tawney stressed equality.[25] Justice as fairness has long been involved in Christian thinking, and in recent years another aspect of justice, concern for the poor, has come into greater prominence. Then, as I have just mentioned, the ecumenical concept of the responsible society and the just, participatory and sustainable society have been put forward as derivatives of the gospel. Sustainable is a new element. It has come to the fore because of the rise of ecological and environmental anxieties but, once it has appeared, it is easy to see that it does not depend on the present context but could be, and would have been, always relevant. All of these might well be called derivative principles from the gospel, to use Temple's term. To say this implies that in principle there should be agreement among Christians that they are derived from the gospels. In practice there are differences among Christians with respect to them, just as there are differences among them on basic aspects of the gospel itself, as presented in the Bible and church tradition; but in principle there is no reason why Christians should not arrive at a broad agreement on both.

Robin Gill maintains that Christians differ more on moral or ideological matters than on technical or specialist ones.[26] This is very doubtful. Certainly they disagree on both. The middle axioms approach and that of Paul Ramsey with his action-orientated principles are designed to reduce their differences on the former, and in principle there is no limit to their success, though in practice complete agreement is unlikely.[27] On technical aspects there is no possibility in principle of complete agreement, and it is very unlikely to be achieved in fact on a detailed issue, if only because of problems in interpreting empirical evidence and the uncertainties inherent in estimating the likely consequences of possible courses of action. Moreover, unless one takes a very deontological view of Christian ethics, such estimates are in many cases involved in deciding on a course of action.

There is the problem of an order of preference between these different 'principles', and that is likely to vary according to varying discernments of the signs of the times. Different contexts require different priorities. The problem of agreeing on these spills over into the next stage of formulating middle axioms. What do they mean concretely at a given time and place? Is it possible for the churches to provide some guidelines based upon some broadly agreed interpretation of the many and confusing movements, crises and causes which jostle in the public forum? Is it possible to indicate what are the significant issues among the welter of issues? What are the trends at the present and for the foreseeable future? What needs encouraging or discouraging? What are the broad possibilities of action and their likely consequences?

It is such questions as these that the formulation of middle axioms is designed to answer. To elucidate these middle range questions means getting at 'the facts' to find out 'what is going on'. Tricky questions arise here because 'facts' are slippery things. Some are apparently clear and straightforward, although even apparently objective statistics can be selective, or notoriously hard to interpret. What stands out as facts worth fixing upon out of the welter of potential detail depends upon criteria of significance which in turn depend upon personal value judgments. Even what is a fact can sometimes depend upon personal interpretation, as anyone who tries to resolve a quarrel between two people soon finds out. Very different accounts are given of the facts behind the quarrel. Again, if we appeal to experts they often differ. Or they may speak with authority beyond their expertise, or have some intellectual or material vested interest which colours their evidence, of which they may be aware, or partly aware, or unaware. I mention these difficulties not in order to discredit the enterprise of forming middle axioms, but to clarify the hazards which have to be faced in doing so. If a church wishes, or churches co-operatively wish, to develop middle axioms in any area they must get together a group of people from relevant disciplines and from those who have practical experience of the issues, for instance as householder, worker, or citizen at whatever level of income and power, privilege or lacking it, to work on the matter.

It is possible that as a result of this co-operative work broad agreement may be reached in suggesting in what direction it is possible to foster change, whilst those who agree on this may differ on the precise policies by which it should be fostered. Christians equally committed to the middle level may well differ on the details of how to further it. A good illustration comes from the 'Butskell' era,[28] when there was a general consensus among Christians that the government should actively maintain full employment. How it should do it involved details of policy on which there was less agreement. Nevertheless the conviction was not an empty one. It presumably began with a judgment, on the level of 'Christian principle', that work is part of the divine intention for man, and that therefore no one should be denied socially significant work by the community. It then went on to an empirical judgment about the record of economic booms and slumps in capitalist societies and decided against a widespread view, dating from the era of laissez-faire, that governments can do little about unemployment. They can only let economic forces do their work. Today that consensus has collapsed (unfortunately, in my view), and any fresh middle axiom on unemployment will have to be worked at from scratch. It might come to the same conclusion!

It may be possible to arrive at a middle axiom on this, or indeed on any particular issue. There is no suggestion that it will always be possible; merely that it is important to try. For instance the role and accountability of transnational corporations has been prominent lately. Their very size makes them conspicuous. There have been enough scandals involving them to cause concern. Yet they have been too easy a target, so that it has been possible for their attackers to avoid awkward questions themselves by putting all blame on TNCs. The WCC since the Nairobi Assembly in 1975 has been investigating them but, having abandoned any middle axiom procedure, gives the impression of paying attention only to hostile evidence. The Board for Social Responsibility of the Church of England set up a small working party on them, whose personnel differed so completely in their opinions (unlike that on nuclear weapons) that its report confined itself to chapters giving contrary positions. No middle axioms were possible.[29] To do no more than this is, however, a service, as far as it goes, because it clarifies the issues. But sometimes when there is no agreement it is possible to go further and, after identifying the main positions held, to ask the Christians advocating each position to sharpen and make explicit the questions they want to raise to those who advocate the other positions. In effect each says to the other: 'We realize that we Christians do not agree on this matter. We respect your integrity and acknowledge that we are bound together in the same faith. But, please, as you maintain in conscience your position consider carefully these questions that we put to you and do justice to them, and we will do the same with the questions you put to us.' The WCC did this fruitfully a decade ago in its work on 'Violence, Non-violence and the Struggle for Social Justice'.[30]

Another way of proceeding has been adopted by the Roman

Catholic Bishops of the USA with respect to the question of nuclear warfare. After a group of them had heard evidence on the matter, the Conference of Bishops produced a draft of a Pastoral Letter which was publicly available for comment in three versions before a final text was issued in May 1983.[31] The Bishops were saying in effect, 'This is what we have in mind to put before the US Government and public. In the light of your reactions we shall produce a final version.' It is an interesting equivalent in an ethical matter of consulting the laity in matters of doctrine, about which Cardinal Newman wrote.[32] Whether, or how far, the final product involves middle axioms, or goes into more precise detailed recommendations, or does both remains to be analysed. It certainly goes beyond generalities.

If the Church of England report on nuclear warfare had confined itself to a middle axiom level it would presumably have been something like, 'Because our general judgment is that the use of even battlefield nuclear weapons will almost inevitably escalate into a full-scale nuclear war which could not be morally justified, the first priority in UK policy should be to work for the abandonment of nuclear weapons.' There are various routes towards the achievement of this, *one* of which is advocated in the detailed proposals of the report. There is no reason why the report could not have listed other feasible ones, with arguments for and against each and between which a choice has to be made, if it had wanted to go further than a middle axiom level. In the event the General Synod voted for a different route from that advocated by the Report, that NATO's strategy of being prepared to use battlefield nuclear weapons first if necessary, to resist a superior attack by conventional weapons, should be abandoned, thereby committing itself to a quite plausible detailed proposal. There is no reason why a Synod should not make such a corporate decision if it is clear on the implications. I make no judgment as to whether the Synod was clear as a result of the debate, but they were not spelled out in the Report.[33]

Once the idea is banished that ethical reflection is like a logical syllogism leading to a clear cut conclusion, it is evident that there are many levels of engaging on moral reasoning in social ethics, which may shade into one another. We need not prescribe precisely how it should proceed, or expect an agreed terminology. The essential point is that it moves from the relatively more certain ground of faith, and 'principles' derived from it, to the less relatively certain ground of empirical analysis and evaluation of 'facts' and trends; and that it attempts to lessen the relativity by seeking by co-operation reflective a consensus at the middle level. It is fully recognized that any individual Christian has to move to some detailed policy conclusion in order to act (so has the church if it wants to act corporately), and that this will involve a much greater degree of uncertainty. In the earlier years of the ecumenical movement this method of church guidance in social ethics was explicitly worked at and successfully put into action. It was perhaps easier when that movement was mainly Western in composition. The more genuinely global it becomes the harder it is to arrive at a consensus, but that does not invalidate the method. In any case it is often necessary to work at less than a global level. There is evidence that the papacy is finding it hard to give universal social teaching in the way that until recently it was assumed that it could, as Paul VI showed in *Octogesima Adveniens*.[34] Nevertheless much work has been done in ecumenical social ethics in this way, even if the term has not been explicitly mentioned. Where it has been abandoned the results are not impressive. In some recent WCC documents there are a number of vague and poorly defined issues, and terms that are little better than slogans, where the concept of middle axioms, or what it stands for, has been abandoned or never heard of.

One of the criticisms of this procedure has been that it is élitist, the equivalent of government by experts. It puts the educated, and especially the academic, in a privileged position. It pays attention to status groups, like scientists, rather than the poor or 'the people' (a term which seems increasingly to be treated as if it refers to a homogeneous entity). These charges could be true, but they are not necessarily so. It is important to draw on the relevant experience of all, especially the poor and those who experience the rough side of life; and not merely to do things for them but to hear them. At the same time there is such a thing as special and technical knowledge without the assistance of which foolish things are likely to be done, with the best intentions. Questions of nuclear energy cannot be dealt with without physicists, or genetical engineering without biologists and medical folk, or work and under-development without economists, even though the issues are too important to be left to them alone. Moreover the trained mind is better able to see the likely secondary consequences of proposed policies, and not only those that are immediately obvious. Grassroots evidence by itself does not settle everything. The relevant contribution of everyone is needed in forming moral judgments in social ethics.

Further criticisms of the middle axioms approach are made by Professor Duncan Forrester.[35] He is not against the concept, but raises cautions and wants to safeguard a distinctively Christian input in the inter-disciplinary process involved in arriving at them. He rightly maintains that the theologian needs to be more than an enabler, an impressario, a catalyst who gets people together and summarizes the results of their work, important as that is. It is also important because non-Christians are often members of such group work, if they are ready to work with Christians, and the church is grateful for their help when their special contribution is needed.

It will be evident from what I have already written that, whilst Christian insights fortunately often overlap with those of other faiths or philosophies, there is no thought of refraining from contributing them when they do not. Indeed they are the basis from which the process of working towards middle axioms starts. However Forrester has a further warning, that this theological contribution may itself spring from an ivory tower misunderstanding of theology; one which presupposes a static, unchanging deposit of faith which is then 'applied' to particular moral issues. Is not *praxis* to be regarded as a criterion of Christian truth[36] I do not think any such presupposition is involved in middle axiom thinking, though those who do have such an attitude to theology might wish to engage in it. Usually, however, such a static view of doctrine goes with a wooden way of 'applying' it rather than the flexible way of middle axioms. It is true that doctrine held cerebrally, with no attempt to live by it, is misunderstood as much as it is understood, and that appreciation comes by the reciprocal relation of *praxis* (if we are to use this Marxist term) and formulations of doctrine, each fertilising the other. Activity and reflection are both necessary. But when we ask what is to be the content of the activity, the problem of answering the question 'What is going on?' is inescapable. If we are muddled or badly mistaken in our answer to it our *praxis* will be unnecessarily defective, and may be harmful. We cannot answer the question from the Bible or the Fathers. We have to get to grips with the data of our own day. Then we are back again at the need for co-operative effort, relevant expertise and experience, and at how far we can get help at the middle level as a stage towards decisions at the detailed level. The liberation theologians, who are the most insistent on *praxis*, realize this and talk of the need for a 'science' to answer the question 'What is going on?' They find it in Marxism. Their realization of a gap to be filled is correct; their method of filling it is mistaken, for Marxism is not such a science. Indeed there is no such science.[37]

Forrester's last criticism is of those who argue that the church should *never* ally itself with a detailed policy option. This is effective against those who make a very sharp distinction between what the church as such may commit itself to and what the individual Christian should. Temple overstated this in *Christianity and Social Order*. It separates the church as such too much from society, giving the impression that it is too detached, too olympian, too free from the hazards of empirical judgment. The church herself is an institution with her own vested interests as an employer of labour and owner of property which are not to be always equated with those of the gospel. Aware of these factors affecting judgments she, too, has to take the risk of making them. Most of the time she does well to remain corporately on the level of middle axioms, thus providing a useful clarification towards personal Christian judgments. But on occasion if there is a significant volume of agreement in her Synods or other representative bodies she may wish to give detailed guidance, as that of the Church of England did with respect to battlefield nuclear weapons. My point is not whether this was a wise decision or not in the circumstances, but merely that in principle it is legitimate for the church on occasion to proceed corporately in this way. But the church must do this in a sufficiently self-critical spirit if she is to seem cogent. Furthermore it should not be done at the expense of exposing the ambiguity and deceptions in public arguments, an important task which a self-critical church should not shirk. The clarifying process of sifting evidence in the effort to arrive at middle axioms is a help in discharging this task.

IV

It is clear that the authority behind a middle axiom must to a large extent depend on the cogency of the process by which it has been arrived at. Church endorsement cannot long cover shoddy work. Moreover any Christian is free to disagree with it; the onus has then shifted on him to produce good reasons for doing so rather than the other way. The fact that some consensus has been arrived at shifts the 'burden of proof' towards the objector. Proof is, of course, a bad word to use, since we are in the realm of probabilities. No one can be sure of the correctness of an analysis of a current situation; no one can be certain of the consequences of encouraging some trends and discouraging others; no one can foresee what will be the effect of unexpected innovations. In matters of ethics as well as of doctrine our pilgrimage is by faith and not by sight. But it is a help to a Christian to have some clarificatory guidance which is more probable than mere opinion, whilst leaving him the essential space for personal decision on details. Those who doubt the wisdom of what is suggested are free to express reasoned alternatives, or to seek them. Nevertheless the broader a consensus the more it should be taken seriously. In this connection the many similarities between the social teaching of the ecumenical movement and of the Roman Catholic Church since Vatican II are very significant.[38]

This links with further points of importance in connection with middle axiom procedure. They root social theology firmly in the realities of the world today. Indeed one of the advantages of a continuous process of developing them is that it forces the churches to keep up to date. The history of social theology has shown how poorly the churches have coped with the dynamic and rapidly changing societies which have followed the Industrial Revolution, and how prone they have been to areaism. It is one of the most valuable results of the ecumenical movement that it has brought the churches up to date in social theology, and markedly improved their chances of remaining so.

Another point is that it forces theologians to work co-operatively with others, since middle axioms cannot be arrived at by theologians on their own. Also, since theologians are usually ordained, it means that the gulf which often exists between ordained and lay is bridged. And again, since a contribution of those of other faiths and ideologies may often be appropriate, it brings Christians into fruitful collaboration with them, and this is of increasing importance in the contemporary world. If the work is successful it gives Christians something well thought out to contribute to public discussion in a plural society. It can often rouse a bad conscience in that society on issues which there has been a public tendency to ignore or to be complacent about. Indeed when one asks what is the factor most likely to govern the choice of issues by the churches on which to work, it is likely to be ones in which an uneasy conscience has begun to develop, so that the process of reflection begins with a negative judgment on the *status quo*. Theoretically, any issue could be worked on, but in practice it is unlikely that any effort will be made in areas in which Christian opinion is (rightly or wrongly) satisfied. Since the evidence is clear that Christian opinion over the centuries has tended to accept the *status quo* too easily, the practice of regarding middle axiom thinking as a main task of Christian social ethics will help to correct this imbalance by increasing an alertness to aspects of the *status quo* on which a negative judgment needs to be passed. Still further, if we are concerned with the unity as well as the renewal of the church, this is a place where, as Oldham stressed, it is especially appropriate for the churches to work together. Little, if anything, is to be gained by working separately; quite the contrary.

Once it is granted that churches as such have a social responsibility, and should give some guidance to their members in exercising theirs, there is a case for thinking that the method of seeking middle axioms in this broad and flexible way is usually the best method of doing so. The deductive methods of proceeding to detailed conclusion from the Bible or Natural Law have broken down. Action for the poor first and reflection afterwards leaves one a prey to slogans and misconceptions. The provisionality inherent in middle axioms is no bar to decisive action, for provisionality is a condition of life itself, and is only disconcerting to those Christians whose faith mistakenly demands certainties, and clear black and white distinctions which life does not normally permit. Sometimes, indeed, a boundary situation is reached where a clear 'No' or 'Yes' must be uttered in the name of God. This is what Paul Ramsey refers to as the 'gateway of Auschwitz situation'.[39] He adds that Christians ought to have been active long before it arose, presumably at the level of what he calls action/orientated principles.

Such a drastic situation, if it is known, cannot be evaded. One of the sad features of the Nazi extermination of the Jews was that many Christians did not know, or did not want to know, or knew but resisted the government only when the church herself was threatened.[40] Racism goes on producing boundary situations. But most of the time we do not live at boundary situations, and short of them, the method of middle axioms is a good one. It is critical of the *status quo*, but it keeps contingent political and social judgments in their proper place, that of the penultimate and not the ultimate.[41] It requires Christian social action and will not sanction a private pietism, but differentiates between God's cause and our causes. It takes the religious overtones out of politics whilst insisting that it is a necessary area of Christian obedience. The fact that we have a long way to go before the Christian community grasps this and follows it is a reason for taking the middle axiom approach seriously and not forgetting it.

There are difficulties involved, but alternative procedures have more. One of the difficulties is that if one lives in a society where opinions are sharply polarized, and if Christians share the polarization, the method is impossible because no consensus can be arrived at. This may also happen on particular issues in societies less polarized in general, as has been the case on the issues of violence and non-violence in the western churches.[42] In that case a useful but more modest course had to be adopted.

We should work to avoid polarization as far as possible, for the more complex the society the less likely is dramatic change to be achieved without much suffering, or to arrive at where those who tried to bring it about by drastic means intended. This is another way of maintaining that the concept of the 'common good' should not be regarded as a chimera but fostered and taken as far as it will go.[43] If polarization does occur no escape from choice exists. There is no neutral ground. Either one supports the existing situation or one is on the side of drastic change. To do nothing is tacitly to support the existing situation. But if we can preserve a society less polarized, and one that does not force us into boundary situations, we are faced with a variety of Christian opinions in the field of social ethics. Our problem is how to clarify the corporate witness of the church whilst leaving voluntary groups to campaign on particular issues,[44] and individual Christians space to make their decisions in their own situations at work and as citizens. To those of a tidy mind the concept of middle axioms, once it has been freed from the mistaken prescriptivist framework, may seem loose and vague. But, to quote the title of a popular television programme, 'That's Life'. As a general method of procedure, allowing that on occasion other methods may be possible or necessary, there seems no better alternative.

Notes

1. The Legacy of the Christian Socialist Movement

1. R. N. Berki, *Socialism*, 1975, ch. 2. He refers (p. 10) to Angelo Rappoport, *A Dictionary of Socialism*, 1924.

2. Berki, op. cit., p. 26.

3. See R. F. Wearmouth, *Methodism and the Struggle of the Working Classes 1850–1900*, 1954, and K. S. Inglis, *Churches and Working Classes in Victorian England*, 1963, which modifies Wearmouth on the influence of Methodism. As a young man I knew the leaders of the Derbyshire Miners' Union in the area where the summer conferences of the Student Christian Movement were held, who were also connected with the Independent Labour Party (more radical than the official Labour Party). The meetings began with 'hymns' i.e., certain church hymns from which theistic references had been removed.

4. But note an unpublished Ph.D. thesis of Edinburgh University by D. F. Summers, 'The Labour Churches and Allied Movements in the Late 19th and Early 20th Centuries', 1958, and K. S. Inglis, op. cit., ch. 6. John Trevor himself had been brought up a Baptist and with a fear of hell. The point of view he came to hold, as expressed in *The Labour Prophet and Labour Church Record* (1892–98), which he edited, was: 'The Gospel of the Labour church is that God is in the Labour movement, working through it for the further emancipation of man from the tyranny, both of his own half-developed nature and of those social conditions which are opposed to his highest development.' Put more crudely, the Labour movement was seen as the focal point of the evolution of God-consciousness.

The Labour churches mostly hired halls for their services/ meetings. Tom Mann, Ben Tillett and Keir Hardie were among itinerant lecturers, though the content of what they said was the same as it would have been at a straight ILP political meeting. On the other hand Conrad Noel was a popular Labour church lecturer, and William Temple took the chair at a Labour church meeting in Leicester in 1907. A Labour Church Union was formed in 1893 and met annually until 1914, but it was a very loose organization, as the churches had a horror of institutionalism, another factor which led to their rapid decline. Scott Holland criticized them for this (and other things) in *The Commonwealth*, November 1896. The revised principles of the Labour churches of 1906 were explicitly not theological and, as a result, John Trevor, who did not die until 1930, lost interest. D. P. Summer's thesis makes clear that the demise of the Labour churches is badly documented.

5. See Raymond Williams, *Keywords*, 1976.

6. In *The Christian Socialist, A Journal of Association*, 25 July 1851.

7. Richard Baxter, *A Christian Directory or a Summ of Practical Theologie and Cases of Conscience*, 1673.

8. His famous Sermon 44 on 'Money' is a good illustration.

9. J. M. Ludlow (1821–1911). Henri de Saint-Simon (1760–1825), Louis Blanc (1815–1882), Charles Fourier (1772–1831). Ludlow was to become from 1875–1891 Chief Registrar of Friendly Societies; see Neville Masterman, *J. M. Ludlow, The Builder of Christian Socialism*, 1963 and *John Ludlow: the Autobiography of a Christian Socialist*, ed A. D. Murray, 1981. The data for a history of the Christian Socialist Movement are seriously incomplete because Ludlow deposited the records at the Working Mens' College, but a secretary of it subsequently destroyed them.

10. Charles Kingsley (1819–1876). He exposed rural conditions in his novel *Yeast*, and sweat shops in another, *Alton Locke*, and in a pamphlet *Cheap Clothes and Nasty*; see Guy Kendall, *Charles Kingsley and his Ideas*, 1946. The quotation is from his *Three Letters to the Chartists*, 1848: 'We have used the Bible as if it were a special constable's handbook – an opium dose for keeping beasts of burden patient while they were being overloaded – a mere book to keep the poor in order. We have told you that the Bible preached the rights of property, and the duties of labour, when (God knows!) for once that it does that, it preaches ten times on the *duties of property* and the *rights of labour*' (p. 58).

11. E. V. Neale (1810–1892). The co-operatives were set up by the Society for Promoting Working Men's Associations, which was closed by Maurice in 1854. Neale later became secretary of the Co-operative Union, and together with Tom Hughes (author of *Tom Brown's Schooldays*) produced the first text book on co-operation, *Manual for Co-operators* in 1881. Hughes was suspicious of consumers' co-operation and the Co-operative Wholesale Society, Neale encouraged them; see P. N. Backstrom, *Christian Socialism and Co-operation in Victorian England*, 1974.

12. The Tailors lasted until 1860, when it collapsed because of a fraudulent manager; and early in the 1860s the Shoemakers were taken over as a private firm. It is thought that Neale lost £40,000 to £60,000 on them. See C. E. Raven, *Christian Socialism (1848–1854)*, 1920.

13. See notes 9 and 11 above. Neale became convinced of the importance of consumer's co-operation (pioneered in Rochdale in 1844), and a Central Co-operative Agency was set up in 1851 to be for consumers what the Society for the Promotion of Working Men's Association was for producers. Ludlow was not very pleased and the Christian Socialists were divided on this.

14. F. D. Maurice (1805–1872). There are many books written about him; perhaps the best for the purpose of the present discussion is M. B. Reckitt, *Maurice to Temple*, 1948.

15. I have dealt with this more fully in the Maurice Lectures, *Religion and the Persistence of Capitalism*, 1979, pp. 69–92. My present references to Calvinism refer, of course, to the immense debate following upon Max Weber's book, *The Protestant Ethic and the Spirit of Capitalism*, 1905. My view of this is also to be found in the Maurice Lectures, pp. 88 ff.

16. Quoted in H. F. Lovell Cocks, *The Nonconformist Conscience*, 1944, p. 35.

17. Quoted in *The Life of Frederick Denison Maurice* by Frederick Morris (his son), 1885, Vol. 2, p. 32.

18. See F. Hirsch, *The Social Limits to Growth*, 1977.

19. In addition to the influence of Maurice, Headlam drew on the Puseyite Tractarian tradition which stressed individual spiritual direction and almsgiving to the poor, but had no significant social theology.

20. Details of these various societies and individuals can be found in S. Mayor, *The Churches and the Labour Movement*, 1967. The COPEC conference or Conference on Christian Politics, Economics and Citizenship at Birmingham with William Temple in the Chair, and 1400 members, was the first large Christian conference in Britain on the social order, and to some extent prepared for the first ecumenical conference on the matter at Stockholm in 1925. See *The Proceedings of COPEC* ed W. Reason, 1924, and the reports of its twelve commissions.

21. See Johnson's *The Socialist Sixth of the World*, 1939, and the Webbs' *Soviet Communism: a New Civilisation?*, 1935.

22. Maurice Reckitt even likened Major Douglas to Einstein, Eddington and Keynes in his *Religion and Social Action*, 1937, quoted by John Orens in *Essays Catholic and Radical* ed K. Leech and R. Williams, 1983, p. 179.

23. Efforts to trace its records have not so far succeeded, though it is not twenty-five years since it came to an end.

24. John Macmurray's *Creative Society*, 1935, was one expression of the Christian left. His Gifford Lectures of 1953 and 1954, *The Form of the Personal*, were to strike a rather different note. Largely

under his influence there was in Canada from 1934–45 a Fellowship for a Christian Social Order which held that capitalism was inherently unchristian and equated the kingdom of God with a socialist commonwealth. The book *Towards a Christian Revolution* ed Gregory Vlastos, 1937, was the best expression of it.

25. I was a member of this group. There was a quarterly journal of the Fellowship of Socialist Christians (USA), founded in 1930 under the influence of Reinhold Niebuhr. He edited the journal, and I was for a time the British agent. It began in 1935 as *Radical Religion* and changed its name in 1940 to *Christianity and Society*, and ceased publication in 1956. The FSC always saw that conflicts of interest would persist in a socialist society. In so far as it took an element of Marxist realism to destroy liberal illusions Niebuhr soon had no need of it. Augustinian realism exposed Marxist illusions. On the other hand Niebuhr's stress on love as self-sacrifice and sin as self-assertion has been thought to be too unqualified as not allowing enough for a proper self-affirmation. (It is a point that men are alleged to underplay, and to forget that women are often not self-affirming enough.) Although Niebuhr ceased to call himself a socialist he never abandoned a belief in equality as a regulative principle by which all structures of justice should be judged. His thought on this theme in the mid-1930s can be found in a chapter 'Christian Politics and Communist Religion' which he contributed to the symposium *Christianity and the Social Revolution* ed J. Lewis, K. Polanyi and D. K. Kitchen, 1935.

26. Its proceedings were published under that title in 1941.

27. Canon Stanley Evans of Southwark Cathedral epitomized the outlook of the Society of Socialist Clergy and Ministers in his book *Return to Reality*, 1955.

28. *The Lamb* was the name of a public house where the group met. I reviewed *Papers from The Lamb* in an article in *Theology* for April 1960, 'The Christian Left Still Lost'. Lord Soper's opinions are expressed in *Christian Politics*, 1977. Stanley Evans wrote another book, *The Social Hope of the Christian Church*, 1965, which expressed the general outlook of the CSM; the kingdom of God is still a corporate society on earth.

29. The Roman Catholic Church is the only major church in England with a strong working-class membership, because of the immigration of labourers from Ireland.

30. Edited by R. Ambler and D. Haslam. I reviewed it in an article 'Not Out of the Wood Yet', in *Theology*, March 1981, the title referring to the article in *Theology* of twenty years earlier (see n. 28 above). The Iona Community in Scotland, and Christian Action, are among the best known groups associated with COSPEC; the former

has been particularly linked with the name of the Revd Dr George MacLeod and the latter with that of Canon John Collins.

31. Gore succeeded Westcott as President of the CSU. His social theology is most conveniently found in an Essex Hall Lecture of 1920, *Christianity Applied to the Life of Men and Nations*, and in his book *Church and Society*, 1927.

32. Vol. XIII, pp. 190–202.

33. In 1917 a private group of which Temple was a member, the Collegium, produced a book *Competition*. *Christianity and Social Order* was a 1942 war-time paperback; the quotation is from the latest reissue of 1976 (pp. 99f.), with an introductory essay by me.

34. I have written about him as a Christian moralist in the Maurice Lectures, pp. 83–110 (see n. 15 above).

35. Raphael Samuel, *Tawney and the SPD*, 1982, a pamphlet published by the Socialist Society.

36. 'Common ownership' is a phrase in the famous Clause 4 of the Labour Party Constitution of 1918. It goes back to the Gotha Programme of the German Social Democratic party of 1878 and the Independent Labour Party in this country in 1890. It was chosen in 1918 as being acceptable to various kinds of socialists (Guild socialism was popular then), and it is open to many meanings, e.g. state shareholdings in capitalist companies, workers' shares in their own companies, workers' representatives on boards of directors (as recommended by the Bullock Report in 1977), consumers' co-operation, producers' co-operation. There are several versions of the last; they have been most successful in agriculture. In industry there are a few long established ones, like Leicester Co-operative Printers, and a number of new small ones furthered by the Industrial Common Ownership Movement, founded in 1975 and the Industrial Common Ownership Finance Act of 1976, as well as the better known ones promoted by Mr Wedgewood Benn, like Triumph Motorcycles at Meriden, Kirby Manufacturing in Merseyside and Scottish News Enterprises in Glasgow, all of which have failed.

37. Cf. my lecture 'The Question of a Just, Participatory and Sustainable Society' in the *Bulletin* of the John Rylands University of Manchester Library, Vol. 63 No. 1, pp. 95–117.

38. Cf. an essay 'Christianity and Self Interest' by Gerard Hughes, SJ, in *Christianity and the Future of Social Democracy* ed M. H. Taylor, 1982.

39. The nationalized Gas industry in the UK is being compelled to raise its prices enormously and to make huge profits as a covert means of raising taxation by a government which came into power pledged to reduce it.

40. See Denys Munby, *Christianity and Economic Problems*, 1956, *passim*.

41. The sources for the Christian Socialist Movement are primarily a large number of pamphlets and periodicals. Among the useful general surveys not already mentioned are A. P. McEntee, *The Social Catholic Movement in Great Britain*, New York 1927; D. O. Wagner, *The Church of England and Social Reform Since 1854*, New York 1930; C. K. Gloyn, *The Church in the Social Order*, Pacific University, Oregon 1942; J. K. Oliver, *The Church and Social Order: Social Thought in the Church of England 1918–1939*, 1968; P. D., A. Jones, *The Christian Socialist Revival 1877–1955*, Princeton 1968; T. Christensen, *The Origin and History of Christian Socialism*, Aarhus 1962: this modifies Raven (n. 12 above) in some respects, but exaggerates the extent to which the Christian socialists won the workers, G. C. Binyon, *The Christian Socialist Movement in England*, 1931. E. R. Norman, *Church and Society in England 1770–1970*, 1976, is useful, especially for the nineteenth century if read with caution.

2. Christianity and Economic Man

1. P. H. Wicksteed, *The Commonsense of Political Economy*, 1910. He was also a Unitarian minister and lifelong friend of John Trevor, the founder of the Labour churches mentioned in the last chapter.

2. G. Becker, *The Economic Approach to Human Behaviour*, Chicago 1977. I once heard the question posed, If twenty people were in an airplane which had to bail out and there were only ten parachutes available, how would economics solve that? The answer is that no economic theory or institution can solve a question on the extreme margin of social existence. Moralists would advance various considerations, including triage and deciding by lot, in the effort to illuminate what actions in such a desperate situation would best express our common humanity.

3. See K. R. Popper, *The Logic of Scientific Discovery*, revd edn 1968, and subsequent discussions of it.

4. Max Weber, *The Methodology of the Social Sciences*, ET New York 1949, and Talcott Parsons, *The Structure of Social Action*, 1937, pp. 601ff.

5. The *General Theory of Employment, Interest and Money*, 1936, p. 383.

6. *The German Ideology*; cf. for example, *Karl Marx, Selected Writings* ed D. McLellan, 1977 p. 169. See Alec Nove, *The Economics of Feasible Socialism*, 1983, for an extended analysis of Marx's economic theories and the problems of the Marxist command economies.

7. Social Credit has now practically faded out. (It turned on the way money circulates in the processes of production in the economic system.) There are issues concerned with our relation to the environ-

ment and with pressures of population which need, and are slowly getting, more attention. The Club of Rome also issued subsequent reports, which modified the first in important respects, but it was the first which caused the sensation and, incidentally, affected a good deal of Christian thinking, including that of the World Council of Churches. One of the best critiques of the issues is that of the Sussex University Policy Research Unit, *World Futures and the Great Debate*, 1978, edited by C. Freeman and M. Jahoda.

8. Sometimes a half-way stage between general values and particular policies can be achieved. See the appendix on 'Middle Axioms in Christian Social Ethics'.

9. And the suggestion of the possibility of a just revolution (Aquinas 'de Regimine Principium' 1.7). Mediaeval economic teaching is conveniently expounded in Viner (n. 12 below).

10. E.g., Ex. 22.25; Deut. 23.19f.; Lev. 25.36f. In the New Testament Matt. 25.27 and Luke 19.23 (but cf. Luke 6.35). Aristotle *Politics* 1.10 1258 B (tr. B. Jowett 1885).

11. *Lucrum cessens* or loss due to failure to repay a loan on time; *Damnum emergens*, or a loss which he actually incurred, by impairment of capital, by lending.

12. *Religion and the Rise of Capitalism*, p. 185 (1929 edition). The development of the scholastic teaching on usury can be studied in B. W. Dempsey, *Interest and Usury*, 1948 and J. T. Noonan, *The Scholastic Analysis of Usury*, 1957 (Roman Catholic authors); also J. Viner, *Religious Thought and Economic Society*, Durham, N. Carolina 1957.

13. *The Wealth of Nations* (Everyman edition, Vol. 1, p. 13).

14. I have discussed the philosophy of possessive individualism in *Religion and the Persistence of Capitalism*, 1979, ch. 4. The return to a seventeenth-century social contract theory of the basis of government in such political philosophers as John Rawls (*A Theory of Justice*, 1930) and Robert Nozick (*Anarchy, State and Utopia*, 1974), is in effect a return to this philosophy but, at least in the case of Rawls, to draw not only libertarian but more egalitarian conclusions from it, on the basis of what kind of society an individual would choose to achieve his greatest advantage, if he had to choose in advance under a 'veil of ignorance' as to what his position in it would be. There is further reference to Rawls and Nozick in chapter 3.

15. A. C. Pigou, *Economics of Welfare*, 1920.

16. In a recent visit to Hong Kong, where a free market system is seen at its most vigorous and dynamic, it was borne upon me that it is underpinned by the strength of the Confucian family system, which it does not realize.

17. Fred Hirsch, *The Social Limits to Growth*, 1977.

18. Bryan Wilson, *Religion in Secular Society*, 1966; *Contemporary Transformations of Religion*, 1976; and the latest one, *Religion in Sociological Perspective*, 1982. The most subtle discussions of secularization are in David Martin, *A General Theory of Secularization*, 1978, and Owen Chadwick, *The Secularization of The European Mind in the Nineteenth Century*, 1975.

19. See W. Grant, *The Political Economy of Industrial Policy*, 1982.

20. Among the many studies of wealth and poverty in Britain two may be singled out; the work of A. B. Atkinson, e.g. *The Economics of Inequality* 1975, and Peter Townshend, *Poverty in the United Kingdom*, 1979. The time spread has also to be considered. The average income of a householder where the main earner is 45–54 is double that where he or she is under 25.

21. J. M. Keynes, *Liberalism and Labour*, 1926.

22. St Thomas Aquinas, *Summa Theologia*, 2, 2: q. 32, 1, 5, 6 and 7, and q. 66, 2, 7.

23. See the discussion in the symposium, *Property: its Duties and Rights*, 1913, with an introduction by Charles Gore and a concluding chapter on 'Property and Personality' by Scott Holland.

24. Marxists are equally hostile to competition. Some of the leaders of the USSR in the early 1920s carried it so far as to advocate communal gymnastics rather than competition in football.

25. *Christianity and Social Order*, 1976 edition, p. 65.

26. See the subtle discussion of 'Christianity and Self-Interest' by Gerard Hughes, SJ, in *Christians and the Future of Social Democracy* ed M. H. Taylor, 1982. Compare also Sermons 11 and 12 of (Bishop) Butler's *Fifteen Sermons* ed T. A. Roberts, 1970.

27. In so far as the Gold Standard ever worked it was because it was thought to be immutable; no one could think so now. Moreover between 1815 and 1914 there were twelve major crises in the USA causing heavy unemployment. The very modest over-all rise in prices in that century was less due to the Gold Standard than the lack of trade unions strong enough to resist wage cuts. There is a further political point, that the two countries that produce most of the world's gold, South Africa and the USSR, have particularly unpleasant governments.

28. Nove, op. cit., p. 60. I am much indebted to Nove for this section. By contrast the analysis of a sophisticated Belgian Marxist economist can be studied in the section on Economics in the symposium, *Marx: the first 100 years* ed D. McClellan, 1983. The clumsy economy of the USSR also completely dominates Comecon, the 10 member Soviet world economic group, and is the reason why it works so badly.

29. Examples of an effort to arrive at a model of a 'democratic' socialist economy include a section in Oscar Lange, *The Economics of Socialism*, ed A. Nove and D. M. Nuli, 1972; Ota Sik, *The Third Way*, ET 1976; and Wlodimierz Bras, *The Market in a Socialist Economy*, ET 1972 and *The Economics and Politics of Socialism*, 1973.

30. See L. Sirc, *The Yugoslav Economy under Self-Management*, 1979.

31. See *Hungary: a Decade of Economic Reform* ed P. Hare, H. Radice and N. Swain, 1981.

32. In the period of the Great Leap Forward and before the Cultural Revolution in China there was an intense debate between the broad and narrow schools of thought on the techniques of economic management, e.g. how should the prices of socialist products be fixed? The narrow school emphasized the essential differences between socialism and capitalism, the broad school more their common elements (even at the risk of being labelled 'revisionist'). After the death of Stalin similar debates surfaced in other Marxist countries. All sides were constrained by having to carry on the debate within Marx's labour theory of value, which decreed that the value of a product is determined by the amount of 'socially necessary labour time' involved in its production.

33. See D. Coates, *Labour in Power: a Study of the Labour Government 1974–79*, 1980.

34. The proportion of the working population in the USA engaged in information jobs increased from 17% to 60% in the thirty years from 1950.

35. For a sceptical analysis of the problem see Dan Usher, *The Economic Prerequisite of Democracy*, 1981.

36. One example. In India 23 million babies are born at present each year. Of these 4 million die in childhood, 9 million suffer severe malnutrition, 7 million lesser malnutrition and only 3 million grow to healthy adulthood. Deficiencies of protein damage the brain and body mechanism from within, and the lack of safe drinking water leads to typhoid and hepatitis. Village health facilities hardly exist, and girls especially often die of neglect.

37. *North-South: a Programme for Survival*, 1980, and *Common Crisis North-South: Co-operation for World Recovery*, 1983.

3. The New Radical Right

1. For instance Copleston wrote on currency questions. There was vision as well as intellectual excitement in the development of economics. Against the narrowness of mercantilism it was argued (often in the context of trade with Ireland) that it was possible for

all nations to grow rich together, and that laissez-faire would enrich the world as a whole, and civilize mankind; this last was a charac-teristic touch of eighteenth and nineteenth century Western self-confidence. Professor Salim Rashid of the College of Commerce and Business Administration in the University of Illinois has for some years been investigating the role of Anglican clergy in the develop-ment of economics. Among his papers there is 'Anglican Christianity and the Growth of Liberal Economics' due to appear in the *Journal of Religious History*, which is specially relevant to this section. He points out that it was the universalist nature of Christian beliefs that led many of them to oppose the idea that one country could prosper only at the expense of another. God could not be supposed to have created a world in which there was a *necessary* conflict between the prosperity of different nations. In this respect a theological convic-tion stimulated in them a development of economic theory.

2. Quoted in *Christianity and Social Order*, 1976 edn, p. 9.

3. *First Essay on Population* (An Essay on the Principle of Population as it Affects the Future Improvement of Society, with Remarks on the Speculations of Mr Godwin, M. Condorcet and Other Writers). Facsimile Reprint by the Royal Economic Society, 1966.

4. *Natural Theology*, 1802.

5. William Whewell, Master of Trinity College, Cambridge, lectured in Mathematics, Minerology and Moral Philosophy, edited Butler's Sermons, translated a drama of Goethe, wrote a major work on the History of Science, and three papers on Mathematical Economics.

6. *A Treatise on the Records of Creation*, 2 vols, 1816.

7. *A Second Letter to The Right Hon Robert Peel MP*, 1819.

8. *Introductory Lectures in Political Economy*, 1831.

9. *On Political Economy*, 1832, and *On the Power, Wisdom and Goodness of God*, Bridgewater Treatise I, 1833.

10. For much of this discussion I am indebted to 'The Ideological Alliance of Political Economy and Christian Theology 1798–1833' by Professor A. M. C. Waterman of the Department of Economics in the University of Manitoba in the *Journal of Ecclesiastical History*, Vol 34, No 2, April 1983, and to the article by Professor Salim Rashid (n. 1 above).

11. The tradition of Christian political economy was continued in the USA in the work of Francis Wayland and Arthur Latham Perry. Protestant clergymen played a prominent part in the early teaching of economics. Francis Wayland's *Elements of Political Economy*, 1837, owed much to Adam Smith and Thomas Chalmers. It was widely used for a generation. John McVickar of Columbia University, one of the first academic economists in the USA, held

that the divinely ordained laws of morality and political economy called for individual responsibility, private property and minimal government interference, and this was generally agreed by clerical economists in the nineteenth century. A. L. Perry's *Principles of Political Economy* appeared in 1891. I owe this information to an unpublished paper 'Clerical Laisser-Faire' by Dr Paul Heyne of the Department of Economics of the University of Washington, Seattle.

12. The term Welfare State seems to have first been used by William Temple in 1941 in his *Citizen and Churchman*, 1941, p. 35. '. . . in place of the conception of the power-state we are led to that of the Welfare State'.

13. Let Paul Johnson (formerly editor of the *New Statesman*) and the educationalist Lord Vaizey stand as representatives. In the USA in 1981 an Institute for Religion and Democracy was founded, with prominent ex-liberals like Michael Novak and Richard John Neuhaus among its backers.

14. I am not suggesting that in either case attitudes were consistent, let alone practices. For instance it is interesting to note how many householders who deprecate state interference and favour privatization at the same time want government action to keep mortgage rates down.

15. *The Road to Serfdom*, 1944.

16. Apart from Hong Kong today.

17. See Anthony Quinton, *The Politics of Imperfection: The Religious and Secular traditions of conservative thought in England from Hooker to Oakeshot*, 1978.

18. The clearest interpretation of original sin known to me is given by William Temple in *Christianity and Social Order*, 1976 edn, pp. 59f.

19. This affirmation is oddly inconsistent with the desire to reduce state provided benefits and appeal to voluntary charity.

20. Cf. *Capitalism and Freedom*, 1962, *passim*. He is a thorough libertarian. His doctrine has a shred of plausibility only with respect to isolated individual adults and heads of families.

21. Cf. the three volumes of *Law, Legislation and Liberty*, *passim* (1973, 1976 and 1979). He is also attracted by the conservative stress on the hidden wisdom of existing institutions.

22. See *A Theory of Justice*, 1971, *passim*.

23. See my *Religion and the Persistence of Capitalism*, 1979, chapter 4.

24. See *Anarchy, State and Utopia*, 1974, *passim*.

25. This has strong echoes of the political economy of John Locke, who stressed the property rights of the individual in that in which he had 'mixed his labour'. *Two Treatises of Government*, 1689 ed P. Laslett 1962; see the Second Treatise, especially chapter 5. Locke,

however, was a mercantilist and not a prophet of modern capitalism. His contention is that an individual's life, liberty and saleable personal property should be free from interference by an absolute, arbitrary, monarch. If Locke's ideas are strictly applied it would mean that the land in Canada belongs to the Indians or the Inuits because no legally valid contracts were made when the white governments appropriated the land. The same would apply in Latin America; there the land belongs to the peasants because it was expropriated by feudal landlords and, even if they subsequently sold it to some other individual or a company, they were selling stolen goods. A few libertarians do argue in this way but they produce no proposals for acting on this admission. For a further reference to Locke see chapter 4, n. 24.

26. See R. Plant, H. Lesser and P. Taylor-Groby, *Political Philosophy and Social Welfare*, 1980, and the article by R. Plant in *Crucible* Jan–March 1983, 'Neo-Liberalism and the Welfare State'.

27. Conservative thinkers tend to explain unrest in society as due to subversives; rather, the surprise is that in an era of large-scale unemployment the oppressed are so patient. See Peter Steinfels, *The Neo-Conservatives*, New York 1979.

28. In so far as duties go with rights there is need for more work on the duties of citizens in a welfare state.

29. E. R. Norman has made similar charges against the clergy of the Church of England in *Church and Society in England 1770–1970*, 1978, and *Christianity and the World Order*, 1974.

30. See, for instance, *Ideology and Utopia*, p. 232.

31. This is the main thesis of V. A. Demant's *Religion and the Decline of Capitalism*, 1952, approaching the issue from a quite different point of view.

32. *Wealth and Poverty*, p. 37.

33. Ibid., p. 23.

34. Ibid., p. 26f.

35. Ibid.

36. Ibid., p. 30.

37. Carnegie was a rare capitalist who embodies Gilder's point. He objected to the institution of the inheritance of wealth and property and held that a capitalist who died with resources to bequeath had failed in his duty of stewardship of wealth.

38. Gilder, op. cit., p. 34f.

39. Ibid., p. 148. But child tax allowances are a good thing.

40. Ibid., p. 38f.

41. Ibid., p. 41f.

42. Ibid., p. 298.

43. Ibid., p. 185.

44. Ibid., pp. 242 and 267.
45. Ibid., p. 206.
46. Ibid., p. 227.
47. See *Capitalism, Socialism and Democracy*, revd edn 1947, *passim*.
48. Ibid., p. 296.
49. More attention needs to be given to Japan which seems to contradict most of the criticisms made by the radical right of the welfare capitalist economy. Japan's successful welfare state is based on higher taxation rates than those in Europe. Its success in curbing a post-OPEC inflation has been due to an active incomes policy, a willingness on all sides to limit job losses and hold down prices, and a very high government deficit due to an investment policy which has stimulated business activity by public expenditure. See Andrew Schonfield, *The Use of Public Power*, 1983, who argues strongly against a polarization of market forces versus government intervention, and maintains that governments must be increasingly interventionist, risk-taking and entrepeneurial.
50. *Quadragesimo Anno*, par. 80.
51. On the other hand Professor P. T. Bauer of the London School of Economics, in an article in the first issue of an American journal, *This World*, 1982, accuses the later Papal Encyclicals *Populorum Progressio* and *Octogesima Adveniens* of encouraging envy, beggary and blackmail: 'An Economist Responds: Ecclesiastical Economics is Envy Exalted'.
52. Canon Peter Selby of Newcastle Cathedral in a semi-private Audenshaw Paper, No. 80, 'The Spirituality of Monetarism', 1981.

4. The Trend to the Left in Twentieth-Century Social Theology

1. Another example of his spirituality is the one hymn he wrote: 'Judge eternal, throned in splendour'; it was for the English Hymnal (1906), of which he was also an editor.
2. H. S. Holland, *Our Neighbours*, 1911, p. 109.
3. See *The New Face of Evangelicalism* ed C. R. Padilla, 1976.
4. Alan Storkey's *A Christian Social Perspective*, 1979, is the best British expression of it so far. He is by training an economist and a sociologist. For information on the Dutch neo-Calvinist tradition I depend very largely on two unpublished papers, one by Bob Gouzwaard, a Professor of Economics at the Free (i.e. Calvinist) University of Amsterdam, and the other by Irving Hexham of the University of Manitoba, Winnipeg, which draws upon his South African experience. Several writings of Gouzwaard are available in English, the most useful perhaps being *Capitalism and Progress*, ET

1979. Troeltsch discussed neo-Calvinism in *The Social Teaching of Christian Churches*, 1931, Vol 2, pp. 655ff. and 935ff. The Dutch Christian Labour Movement is discussed in M. P. Fogarty, *Christian Democracy in Western Europe*, 1957; Peter Drucker , *The End of Economic Man*, 1939, reflects neo-Calvinism.

5. It was in fact Luther even more than Calvin who stressed the doctrine of the Calling and of the office (German *stand*). See, for instance, Gustaf Wingren, *The Christian's Calling : Luther on Vocation*, 1958.

6. These Christian parties are on the wane now in Holland. Alan Storkey stood as a Christian Party candidate in the UK 1974 General Election.

7. The early stages of the social ethics of the Ecumenical Movement can be studied in *A History of the Ecumenical Movement* ed R. Rouse and S. Neill, 1954, chs. 11, 12; H. E. Fey, *The Ecumenical Advance 1948–68*, 1970; Norman Goodall, *Ecumenical Progress, a Decade of Change in the Ecumenical Movement*, 1971, and Ans J. van der Bent, *The Utopia of World Community*, 1974. See also C. C. West, *The Power to be Human : Towards a Secular Theology*, New York 1971 and Paul Bock, *In Search of a Responsible World Society*, Philadelphia 1974.

8. *The Churches Survey Their Task*, 1937, introduced by J. H. Oldham, pp. 87–129.

9. The debt of the ecumenical movement to this great and modest man can easily be overlooked and his name forgotten. A biography has been on the way for several years and it is to be hoped it reaches completion.

10. The nature of this concept and the modifications needed in it is best studied in ch. 3 (by Egbert de Vries) of *Technology and Social Justice* ed R. H. Preston, 1971. See also E. Duff, *The Social Thought of the World Council of Churches*, 1954. A thorough study of the social ethics of the WCC in this period is C.-H. Grenholm, *Christian Ethics in a Revolutionary Age*, Uppsala 1973; cf. M. Lindqvist, *Economic Growth and the Quality of Life*, Helsinki 1975.

11. The report was published by the WCC in 1967 under the title *World Conference on Church and Society*.

12. The Report was published by the WCC in 1980 in two volumes, *Faith and Science in an Unjust World*, Vol 1 ed R. Shinn, Vol 2 ed P. Abrecht.

13. Some account of it is given in *Anticipation*, No 26, June 1979, an occasional bulletin of the Department on Church and Society, reprinted in *Ecumenism and the New World Order* ed M. Arruda, 1980, which also includes the reports of two meetings of a small Advisory Group on Economic Matters created by the Churches' Commission on Participation and Development of the WCC on its own (it had jointly sponsored the Zurich Consultation with Church and Society).

Its pre-occupations cover the same ground as the Brandt Commission, though its many detailed and useful suggestions tend to be more radical. In its general theological, economic and political analysis, however, it is very uneven, tending to talk rather naively of international co-operation as against competition, and of a 'Just, Participatory and Sustainable Society' with respect to 'the peoples' participation' in a way which avoids basic economic and political problems. An example is a quotation from p. 83, where it is talking about a redistribution of the world's wealth and says 'it would require new, but reliable and regular, political processes and instruments. Institutions of central planning and administration would have to be controlled through political processes that effectively incorporate methods of ensuring peoples' participation'. Such a statement of an ideal which it is hard to disagree with, without any indication of the next possible moves forward in terms of the current political tendencies, is precisely the kind of church statement about which Dr J. H. Oldham protested in the formative years of the ecumenical movement, and which led him to write of the need to develop 'middle axioms' (see Appendix 2).

14. See *Anticipation*, No 19, November 1974.

15. Held in Cyprus in 1981. The two quotations are from the privately circulated report. It was published, with much other material, in *Perspectives on Political Ethics* ed Koson Srisang, Geneva and Georgetown, Washington DC 1983. Among it is a short section by Roger Hutchison and Gibson Winter, 'Towards a Method in Political Ethics', which is an important illustration of a trend in WCC social ethics discussed within this section. Unfortunately it appeared only just before work on this book had to finish and could not be used in this chapter. Hutchison and Winter accept without criticism 'the People's story' as a basic concept, and examine the problem of understanding this 'story' along the lines of Ricoeur's method of arriving at an understanding of a literary text. There are three stages. First one 'guesses' what genre it is as a whole, next one analyses it, and lastly one comprehends its disclosure power. The difficulty, they maintain, is that analytical models usually arise from a Western pattern of thought and action, one of understanding, prediction and control, and this excludes 99% of the people. Gramsci struggled with this, and coined the term 'organic intellectuals' for those who identified with and shared the struggles of the people, as distinct from traditional intellectuals. They say 'The wisdom of the People provides the one sure resource for creative ethical work. The People constitute the ethical reality of the total society, for they are the bearers of the possibility of overcoming oppression in the name of justice and peace' (p. 166). They come to

the familiar conclusion of the liberation theologians that 'religious confessions' must contribute to the political responsibility of the People in shaping the future. Only so can they challenge its aberrations; whereas in fact they want to play this critical role without sharing the struggle of the People or understanding their oppression and suffering (p. 168).

It is necessary to disentangle the valid points from the dubious ones in this. (1) the concept of the People (it always has a capital P) needs critical examination; (2) the analytical problem of the relation of experts to the People need not be quite so unresolved; the discussion of middle axioms in Appendix Two bears on this; (3) the theological utopianism implied in the two quotations from p. 166 needs theological correction; (4) there is much truth in the sentences from p. 168, which I have summarized.

16. See, for instance, M. Arruda (ed), *Ecumenism and a New World Order: The Failure of the 1970s and the Challenge of the 1980s*, WCC 1980, pp. 18ff. (see n. 13 above).

17. One defect in the consultation work is that there has been very little contact with the trade union movement, at least in the West where I have most knowledge. This is because trade unionists are minimally related to the churches (but not much more so than natural scientists, who have now been drawn in on the energy issue). The result is that the radical ideas have come from middle-class radicals, who are generally more theoretical and 'pure' in their theories than working-class folk, involved as they are in what are to them the vital details of organized labour and trade union activity. The bulk of the middle class who are not radical tend, perhaps because they are in the middle, to think that properly understood there are no conflicts between owner and worker, and manager and managed, which cannot be overcome with goodwill and reason; and that industrial and economic life is a positive sum game. This kind of thinking has never had much influence in WCC consultations.

18. As one example see the Report of Section I of the World Conference on Mission and Evangelism at Melbourne, *Your Kingdom Come*, 1980.

19. The method of ecumenical social ethics has its importance. I have described this in ch. 1 of *Technology and Social Justice* in connection with the nature of the Consultations (which speak *to* but not *for* the churches), the selection and nature of the people composing them, the conditions of work at them, and the type of report they produce. Sometimes they get no further than a consensus on the issues at stake, but not on strategies for dealing with them; sometimes they go further and define the areas of disagreement and raise

questions which those on each side of an issue wish to put to those who take a different view. Sometimes they can go even further and reach agreement on the general direction in which to move; this is the level of middle axioms (see Appendix 2). Only in the rarest and most clear cut cases is it likely that a complete agreement on details of policy can be commended to the churches. The inter-disciplinary nature of the whole procedures are most important, and the WCC has developed a good technique in using it.

20. See 'The Ecumenical Commitment to a Transforming Social Justice' in *Continuity and Discontinuity in Church History* ed F. F. Church and T. George, Leiden 1979.

21. *Aeternae Patris*, 1879.

22. par. 15.

23. par. 26.

24. Locke argues in ch. 5 of the *Second Treatise of Government*, 1689 that (1) the earth is given to mankind in common; (2) everyone has a property in his own person and that includes his labour; (3) so what he removes out of the state of nature and mixes his labour with becomes his own property. But there are three provisos: (1) enough is left for others; (2) no more is taken than can be used before it spoils; (3) only what one can produce by his *own* labour can be taken. This teaching could equally well be taken as a criticism of most systems of private property rather than a defence of their inviolability. See an article by A. M. C. Waterman, 'Property Rights in John Locke and in Christian Social Teaching' in *Review of Social Economy*, Vol XI, No 2.

25. par. 14.

26. *Rerum Novarum*, par. 28.

27. Ibid., par. 62.

28. According to Oswald von Nell-Breuning, SJ, who was the sole Papal Consultant. He adds that it now seems 'frighteningly irresponsible' to have produced an official document in this way with no significant counter check, and that an international group of recognized specialists in the sciences should participate in the elaboration of such statements; cf. the article 'Octogesima Anno' in *Stimmen der Zeit*, 187, 1971, pp. 289–296 (quoted by R. A. McCormick in *Theological Studies*, March 1982, p. 96).

29. Notably his *True Humanism*, ET 1938.

30. See M. Fogarty, *Christian Democracy in Western Europe*, 1957.

31. Part 5. John XXIII's Encyclical *Mater et Magistra*, 1961, which as its date implies was another commemoration of *Rerum Novarum*, and modified slightly its teaching on private property by appealing more to the principle of subsidiarity of *Quadragesimo Anno* to establish individual and group freedoms. But its method is

different from that of the 1931 Encyclical and anticipates that of Vatican II and after.

32. paras 8, 9, 20, 33, 58, 60.

33. paras 31ff.

34. par. 8.

35. par. 14.

36. par. 14.

37. Another indication of differences of judgment on these matters is shown by the publication in 1982 of the large authoritative text-book *The Social Teaching of Vatican II* by Rodger Charles, SJ, with Drostan MacLaren, SJ. Fourteen pages are given to the Puebla Conference and none to Medellín, and the statement *Justice in the World* of the Synod of Bishops in Rome in 1974 is not mentioned, whereas the concluding address of the Pope to the 1980 Synod (widely thought to be disappointing) is.

38. There has been a similar shift in Lutheranism towards a much more flexible use of the Two Realms doctrine instead of the traditional overwhelming support of the *status quo*. See K. H. Hertz, *Two Kingdoms and One World*, Minneapolis 1976.

39. There is not, of course, uniformity among liberation theologians. Miranda is one of the most naive in holding that the Christian gospel involves a classless society in which all is held in common, and that Marxism is only an incident in the history of Communism. See *Marx against the Marxists*, 1978, and *Communism in the Bible*, 1982.

40. In an article in the American fortnightly *Christianity and Crisis*, 17 September 1973, p. 175.

41. Both strands are found in Bonino's *Toward a Christian Political Ethics*, 1983.

42. The best introduction amid the large literature on liberation theology is still G. Gutierrez, *A Theology of Liberation*, ET 1973. Two others are J. L. Segundo, *The Liberation of Theology*, ET, NY 1975 and J. Andrew Kirk, *Liberation Theology*, 1979.

5. Problems of Prophecy

1. A classic exposition of Functional Sociology is Talcott Parsons, *The Structure of Social Action*, 1937 and, to a lesser extent, Robert K. Merton, *Social Theory and Social Structure*, 1949.

2. For an account of sociological aspects of the ministry of Jesus see Gerd Theissen, *The First Followers of Jesus; A Sociological Analysis of the Earliest Christianity*, 1978.

3. See the classic treatment in H. Richard Niebuhr, *Christ and Culture*, 1952.

4. In the Priestly tradition of the Old Testament there is the Noachian covenant (Gen. 9.8–17) and in the J. tradition the Abrahamic covenant (Gen. 15.17ff.). The dominant tradition, however, looks back to the Mosaic covenant; and it is to this that the prophets look back (Amos 3.1ff.; Hosea 2.15; Jer. 7.22–6; Ezek. 16.3–8 etc.). Jer. 7.23 is a succinct statement of its formal content; the new covenant is outlined in Jer. 31.31ff. (cf. Ezek. 16.60ff.).

5. A concise treatment of common morality is to be found in the Appendix ('Illustrations of the Tao') to C. S. Lewis' Riddell Lectures of 1943, *The Abolition of Man*, 1944.

6. Jer. 1.4–10.

7. Eg. Ezek. 22.12.

8. Eg. Hosea 4.14.

9. Eg. Isa. 30.15–17, 31.1; Hosea 10.13.

10. Eg. Isa. 10.12–16; Jer. 50.31, 51.25–49.

11. Amos 5.14 and Isa. 16.3–8 are examples of the exceptions.

12. *The Sixteen Revelations of Divine Love*, the Lady Julian of Norwich; a fourteenth-century mystic whose dates are uncertain.

13. Nehemiah was in charge of the rebuilding of the walls of Jerusalem *c* 444 BC.

14. See 'Reflections on Theologies of Social Change', esp section IV, in *Theology and Change* ed Ronald H. Preston, 1975; reprinted in *Religion and the Persistence of Capitalism*, 1979.

15. Note especially the Acclamations in The Order for Holy Communion (Rite A) in *The Alternative Service Book 1980*: 'Christ has died: Christ is risen: Christ will come again.' It is the same in all four Eucharistic Prayers and there is no alternative, unlike the new Roman Catholic liturgies.

16. Jer. 32.7ff.; among other examples are Isaiah 20 and Hosea's marriage (Hos. 1).

17. Eg. Isa. 28.7; Jer. 14.14, 28.15.

18. Eg. Jer. 2.8; 23.10.

19. Eg. Jer. 28.9.

20. Eg. Zech. 13.4–6; Mal. 4.5–6; I. Macc. 4.46.

21. There are many treatments of the kingdom of God in the teaching of Jesus; among them Norman Perrin, *Jesus and the Language of the Kingdom*, 1976, may be singled out.

22. The prophecies of Third Isaiah (chs. 56–66) in their expectations exhibit a transition between prophecy and apocalypic.

23. Eg. Acts 10.44, 19.6.

24. Eg. Acts 13.1, 21.8.

25. Eph. 4.1–16.

26. I Thess. 5.19–22; I Cor. 12.4–7, 27–31, 14; Rom. 12.3–8; Eph. 4.11–16.

27. *Didache* 11–13.

28. Isa. 10: 5ff. and other passages.

29. Jer. 25.9 and other passages; Hab. 1.6.

30. Isa. 44.28, 45.1.

31. An example is the claim in *The Witness of the Jews to God* ed D. W. Torrance, 1982, that the return of the Jews to Israel is a fulfilment of prophecy, that Israel's military success is a sign of God's favour, and that encountering Israel is to encounter God and be judged by him (pp. 154ff.).

32. The New Testament talks of two ages, St Augustine of Two Cities and Luther of Two Realms or Kingdoms, variants and developments of the same basic idea.

33. See especially Victor Paul Furnish, *The Love Command in the New Testament*, 1972; and for a wider study Gene Outka, *Agape: An Ethical Analysis*, 1972.

34. See Reinhold Niebuhr, *Moral Man and Immoral Society*, an early work of 1932 but first published in Britain only in 1963, and remaining of fundamental importance.

In this connection the problem of prejudice among Christians arises: see R. L. Gorsuch and D. Abshire, 'Christian Faith and Prejudice: Review of Research', in *Journal for the Scientific Study of Religion*, Vol 17, No 3, 1974. It shows, for instance, that in the USA lay churchgoers were more anti-semitic and racially prejudiced than either clergy or the non-churchgoing public.

35. Paul Tillich, *Love, Power and Justice: Ontological Analyses and Ethical Applications*, 1954, is a classic treatment.

36. M. M. Thomas, an outstanding lay Christian leader in the Mar Thoma Church of South India and in the World Council of Churches, wrote in *Christian Participation in Nation Building*, Christian Institute for the Study of Religion and Society, Bangalore, India 1964: 'In the modern world it is impossible to conceive of any particular moral or Christian responsibility in politics, economics or society without involving ourselves in technical problems which are rarely simple and clear. One may go further and say that it is in the technical decisions that one is moral or immoral and Christian or non-Christian. And without an understanding of the technical issues that are involved in the field in which Christians are called to act responsibly, mere goodwill or even piety does not go far' (p. 297).

37. A. D. Lindsay, *The Two Moralities: Our Duty to God and to Society*, 1940, is a good presentation of this point.

38. Detailed policies also involve a decision as to whether, having defined the facts of the situation, we are going to act according to a

rule of conduct or by an estimate of the best likely consequences of possible actions, evaluated by criteria drawn from our Christian faith; in other words whether to act deontologically or teleologically. In practice either position can be regarded as a norm from which the other may be taken on occasions as an exception. Most of the time we follow rules which we have been taught and/or arrived at ourselves, until an unusual situation crops up which causes us to doubt whether the rule is right for the occasion or whether we should decide according to estimated consequences. This was the subject of the 'situation ethic' debate of the mid-sixties to the mid-seventies, of which the main effect, whether acknowledged or not, was to modify some of the more rigid rule-bound attitudes among Christians.

39. Privately circulated.

40. Jürgen Moltmann is a good example. In 'The Christian Theology of Hope and its Bearing on Development', a paper for a Consultation on 'In Search of a Theology of Development' called in 1969 by Sodepax (a joint activity of the WCC and the Pontifical Justice and Peace Commission), he contrasts the calculable future, which can be extrapolated from present trends, and the anticipated future (*l'avenir*) belonging to the realm of the parousia. He argues that the stress on the first smothers man's wishes in calculations.

41. Quoted in *Crucible*, The Journal of the Board for Social Responsibility of the General Synod of the Church of England, July–September 1982. A good example of simple identification of God's cause with our causes is the remark of Richard Cobden in 1846 that the repeal of the Corn Laws was 'the most important event in history since the coming of Christ'; quoted in Donald Read, *Cobden and Bright: A Victorian Political Partnership*, 1967 p. 65.

42. Robin Gill, *Prophecy and Praxis*, 1981. 'Churches, as churches, can be prophetic in society only in the most unusual circumstances. Usually their relationship to particular societies is too close to allow them to be independently prophetic' (p. 59). Only in the long term and in a general way does he think they can be prophetic.

43. For example, the Roman Catholic Archdiocese of Birmingham.

44. A classic work on this theme is that of the Marxist Ernst Bloch, *Das Prinzip Hoffnung*, 2 vols, Frankfurt 1959, which regrettably has never been translated into English. There is a good treatment of Bloch in James Bentley, *Between Marx and Christ*, 1982, esp. ch. 5. Bloch's point is not the one I am making but not one I deny. He is concerned with the importance of utopias as a counterweight to ideologies of the *status quo*, and a stimulus to transform the present. Theologians influenced by him have been concerned with whether what he wanted is plausible without the faith in God which he

repudiated. My concern is a different point, that utopias need the scrutiny of a prophetic religion.

45. Alistair Kee's *Seeds of Liberation* (the writing up of a conference in Huddersfield of the Student Christian Movement in 1973), where he suggests radical Christian groups should temporarily withdraw from the political struggle and build up alternative life-styles based on eucharistic communities; and his *A Reader in Political Theology*, 1974, ends with an excerpt from Thomas Merton's *Contemplation in a World of Action*, 1971.

46. See Frank Wright, *The Pastoral Nature of the Ministry*, 1980, ch. 7.

6. *Politics, the Church and the Gospel in the Late Twentieth Century*

1. See the discussion of Marxist economics in the second chapter.

2. This has been argued by, e.g., Ota Sik and Oskar Lange. See the discussion in chapter 2, section 3.

3. *The Destiny of Man*, 1937, p. 120.

4. Cf. Isaiah 44.9–18.

5. In the first essay, 'Capitalism, Democracy and Christianity' in *Christians and the Future of Social Democracy* ed M. H. Taylor, 1982.

6. *The Radical Tradition*, 1964, p. 168.

7. See chapter 4, 'Capitalism, Socialism, Personal Freedom and Individualism' in my *Religion and the Persistence of Capitalism*, 1979.

8. *Christianity and the World Order*. Dr Norman ricochets between stressing 'the evocation of the unearthly' as the essence of Christianity (p. 79), and approval of the ages when it sacralized politics, and the clergy occupied a position of confidence and privilege within the structure of the state (p. 4), though he would not want to equate the latter position with the gospel as he accuses the advocates of 'liberal' causes of doing.

9. I am, however, dubious about drawing a social doctrine from the nature of God in himself (as distinct from what we understand of what is disclosed to us) i.e. from a doctrine of the social Trinity. There are dangers of tri-theism here. The doctrine of the Trinity strains the bounds of language, though it is necessary because (as St Augustine said) we cannot be silent on the matter. But we must not claim to know so much about the mystery of the Godhead as to be able to base an ideal model of a social order on that knowledge.

10. There has been a recent tendency of theology to follow the greater environmental and ecological preoccupations and elaborate a theology of nature which gives man a less distinctive place. Nature can be referred to as man's sister or partner. The intention to warn

against human brashness is admirable; the doctrine proposed needs criticism.

11. The Sermon of the Mount (Matt. 5–7) *passim*, especially Matt. 6.

12. E.g., St Paul in Gal. 5.28–9.

13. Ninian Smart, *The Phenomenon of Christianity*, 1979, is a good survey.

14. Peter Hinchcliffe, *Holiness and Politics*, 1982. One of its main themes is the relation of holiness to the rough and tumble of politics, its pressures and constricted choices.

15. Luke 12.16–21, 16.19–31; Matt. 6.25–34; Mark 10.24ff. and many other passages. There is probably some apocalyptic expectation behind these passages, suggesting that questions of riches become irrelevant at the parousia, but it does not affect the permanent significance of concern for the poor.

16. See David Mealand, *Poverty and Expectation in the Gospels*, 1980, and Martin Hengel, *Property and Riches in the Early Church*, ET 1974.

17. For example the argument of Charles Birch and John B. Cobb Jnr, *The Liberation of Life*, 1981, is that the concept of growth needs to be replaced by that of sustainability, and that the constraints imposed by our finite environment are 'not challenges to be overcome but limits to be respected' (p. 236). In so far as there are limits they must of course be respected, and there must be some, but economically we have little idea what they are.

18. Growth arises out of new discoveries, the technological invention of new materials, technical developments which allow lower grade materials to be used, the extraction of hitherto inaccessible materials, and the discovery of new sources of old materials. As far as innovation is concerned the micro-chip revolution may be signalling a move away from the era of giant industrial companies. It has been suggested that two-thirds of the major inventions in the last fifty years have come from individuals or small firms, e.g., air conditioning, automatic transmissions, jet engines, ballpoint pens, penicillin, xerography, zippers (*The Economist*, 17.4.82); crease resistant fabrics, float glass and synthetic detergents came from big companies. Command economies are not good at innovation in factories or farms.

19. Dehydration because of diarrhoea can now be treated by the right proportion of salt and glucose dissolved in water (instead of an intravenous saline drip); vaccines have been developed which immunize, but do not require refrigeration; and the cheapening of communications media could facilitate education for breast feeding in the Third World.

20. The Brandt Report, *North-South: a Programme for Survival*,

1980, tries to show that its proposals would be in the self-interest of the West but does not develop the point made here, perhaps because it was too politically delicate. On the other hand radical critics of the Report who maintain it merely bolsters corrupt regimes in the Third World are in danger of paternalism, and of making the best the enemy of the good. Of course Third World countries have to put their own houses in order, e.g., Ghana and Nigeria do not pay their farmers enough for their crops and make imports artificially cheap by maintaining over-valued currencies. This subsidizes cities, which are growing too fast, and increases the influence of people with import licences (often related to politicians).

21. His *After Virtue*, 1981, contains in chapter 8 a good treatment of this point, on which I have drawn.

22. Gilder, op. cit., pp. 117f.

23. See n. 49 on Japan in chapter 3.

24. See n. 35 below.

25. See the book of that title by David Sheppard, Bishop of Liverpool, 1983.

26. Lev. 25.

27. The American Declaration of Independence of 1776 affirms that it is self-evident 'that all men are created equal'. The roots of this far from self-evident conviction came both from Stoicism, whose logic found it hard to convince others, and from the Judaeo-Christian tradition where it has a stronger base.

28. New Series, Vol XXV, No 1, 1982, p. 67.

29. See *The German Ideology: Theses on Feuerbach*, and the Preface to the *Critique of Political Economy*, 1859.

30. There is a considerable literature on the Sociology of Knowledge, but its bearing on theology is most succinctly expressed in a chapter by Nicholas Lash, 'Theory, Theology and Ideology' in *The Sciences and Theology* ed A. R. Peacocke, 1981.

31. In *Agenda for Prophets* ed Rex Ambler and David Haslam, 1980, pp. 102ff.

32. Orthopraxis is often set up as the criterion rather than orthodoxy, influenced by the Marxian concept of the unity of theory and practice. This is misleading. In the Christian faith there is always a gulf between theory and practice, between what in my own case I know ought to be and what is. My faith needs scrutiny by a theology which at the same time allows itself to be called in question.

33. Professor Kenneth Medhurst and Dr George Moyser have for some years been investigating the social composition and opinions of the General Synod of the Church of England, as an example of middle-class attitudes. See 'Patterns of Representation in the elections to the General Synod of 1975' (*Crucible*, April 1979) and 'The

1980 General Synod: Patterns and Trends' (*Crucible*, April 1982), both by Moyser; 'Political Parties and Attitudes in the Church of England' (*Government and Opposition*, Jan. 1982 and 'The Political Organization of the Middle Class: The Case of the Church of England' in *The Middle Class in Politics* ed J. Garrard 1978, by Medhurst and Moyser. They have also studied the episcopate in 'From Princes to Pastors: The Changing Position of the Anglican Episcopate in English Society and Politics' in *Western European Politics*, May 1982.

34. An interesting example comes from California after the passing of Proposition 13 in 1978. Voters were supposed to be rebelling against government spending and taxation levels, but when presented with a list of government programmes a majority favoured the *status quo* in spending or increased spending, both federal and local. Welfare, foreign aid and food stamps were unpopular, but welfare services to the elderly and handicapped were popular but not those to low income families with dependent children. Benefits in principle available to everyone were favoured as against those which were selective; in short the voters wanted reduced taxes and at the same time favoured the most costly services. See D. O. Sears and J. Citrin, *Tax Revolt: Something for Nothing in California*, 1982.

35. Frank Field, *Inequality in Britain: Freedom, Welfare and the State*, 1982. The other four Welfare States he identifies are (1) The Allowance State; (2) The Company Welfare State (for executives); (3) The Unearned Income State; (4) The Private Market State. The more affluent one is the more one benefits from them.

36. R. Plant, H. Lesser and P. Taylor-Gruby, *Political Philosophy and Social Welfare*, 1980.

37. The chapter on 'Sociology' by Tom Bottomore in *Marx: The First 100 Years* ed D. McClellan 1983 illustrates the new situation which Marxist sociology has to interpret, its varied ways of doing so in the last twenty-five years, and the difficulties it has faced in doing so (though he does not connect these with economic doctrines). The chapter on 'Economics' by Ernest Mandel in the same book is a good example of the convolutions involved in still writing within the traditional Marxist economic categories.

38. Amid the vast literature on Christianity and Marxism see James Bentley, *Between Marx and Christ*, 1982; and A. J. van der Bent, *Christians and Communists*, 1980. On liberation theology see the books mentioned in n. 42 of chapter 4.

39. *Religion in Sociological Perspective*, 1982, chapter 2.

40. See S. M. Beer, *Britain Against Itself: The Political Contradictions of Collectivism*, 1982. A similar problem arises over the Brandt Reports' proposals (see above), membership of the EEC, and the

drift to protectionism. The benefits of freer trade are diffuse and long term, and therefore do not secure a powerful lobby behind them, whereas the disadvantages to particular groups are immediate and possibly traumatic.

41. *Political Theology and the Life of the Church*, ET 1978, pp. 120ff.

42. Alasdair MacIntyre, *After Virtue*, especially chapter 17, but it is the theme of the whole book. The virtues he stresses are courage, honesty and constancy. Others which might be suggested are patience and hope. See also John Finnis, *Natural Law and Natural Rights*, 1980.

43. Ludwig Wittgenstein, *Philosophical Investigations*, 1953, par. 65–77.

44. Op. cit., MacIntyre, pp. 236ff.

45. *Seeds of Liberation*, 1973, pp. 112f.

46. It is in this context that the question whether churches should symbolically disinvest in South Africa is raised. Which is the better course, progressive disengagement or constructive engagement? In either case it is important not to let this issue obscure the fact that the decision is a small part of what the British churches need to do to combat racism, which is latent in much of their membership.

47. *Into the City*, 1982.

48. Ibid., p. 134.

49. Ibid., p. 137.

50. Ibid., p. 53.

51. Ibid., p. 128.

52. *The Church and its Function in Society*, part 3.

53. G. S. Ecclestone, *The Church of England and Politics: Reflections on Christian Social Engagement*, 1980.

54. The phrase is the title of a book on the sociology of religion by Peter Berger, published in the USA as *The Sacred Canopy*, and in Britain as *The Social Reality of Religion*, 1969.

55. It has been shrewdly said that one problem of the Roman Catholic Church in Poland is that it is powerful but denied responsibility; so it can too easily disclaim responsibility and claim innocence.

56. This raises once more the question of how far it is possible for the church on most issues to get beyond generalities without endorsing the details of policy, which is discussed in Appendix 2. It also raises the question of the processes in dealing with politics. A good example of how not to proceed in either respect is provided by the phenomenon of the 'Nonconformist conscience', which was a prominent feature of the political life of the UK between the Franchise Acts of 1867 and 1918, and was at its zenith between

1874 and 1905. It had four characteristics: (1) a political policy was given unqualified religious endorsement, (2) it was promoted by campaigns and demonstrations such that at any one time only one issue could be given attention, (3) the tactics were entirely negative; no negotiation was possible because that would be parleying with unrighteousness (the Devil had to have visible horns and hooves), (4) the emphasis on the sins of others produced a moral complacency in those who denounced them. An anonymous pamphlet in 1909 pointed out some of these weaknesses. It faded out with the decline of political liberalism (Labour was not interested), and then made another mistake by turning to what were thought to be a-political issues of personal morality such as temperance (usually meaning total abstinence), gambling and Sunday observance. Moreover the arguments in all three cases were weak, but that is another issue. See for example, D. W. Bebbington, *The Nonconformist Conscience: Chapel and Politics 1870–1914*, 1982.

57. 'Tawney and the SDP', 29 March and 5 April 1982.

58. How a greater economic equality can be achieved by various taxation policies concerning income and wealth and better access for all to adequate housing, health and education facilities, are matters of detailed discussion. So are better systems of management and participation in decision making in industry. The polarization of social democracy versus democratic socialism seems less and less useful in advanced industrial societies.

59. There is a typology of levels of religious commitment in Gerhard Lenski, *The Religious Factor*, 1961, refined by G. Glock and R. Stark in *Religion and Society in Tension*, 1965, whilst R. Bellah stresses the privatization of religion in a pluralist modern industrial society in *Beyond Belief: Essays on Religion in a Post-Traditional Society*, 1970. It is important that the religion should not be private in the sense of a solitary, mute mysticism.

60. Richard Dickinson, *Poor, Yet Making Many Rich: The Poor as Agents of Creative Justice*, Geneva 1983.

Appendix 1

1. The most thorough typology of sects by sociologists of religion, who are fascinated by them, is that of Bryan Wilson, especially his *Religious Sects: a Sociological Study*, 1970, where he has a seven-fold classification. It is doubtful, however, whether some of the Christian minority communities fit into any of the seven types.

2. Even the Levellers excluded workers for pay and small tenant farmers from voting.

Appendix 2

1. January 1971 : it is the journal of the Board for Social Responsibility of the general Synod of the Church of England.
2. Report of a WCC Consultation on Ecumenical Perspectives in Political Ethics, Cyprus 1981. But in an Introductory paper for the Consultation, published with the report in *Perspectives on Political Ethics*, Konrad Raiser of the General Secretariat of the WCC says 'It is my personal conviction that the very early proposal of J. H. Oldham to work out "middle axiom" (*sic*) or intermediate criteria still has value today and that, in fact, we have followed this direction in many other areas of ethical concern.' It becomes clear, however, that he understands them more like Paul Ramsey's action-orientated principles. See section IV of this Appendix, and chapter 4, n. 15.
3. 'A Second Look at Middle Axioms'. The *Annual* is edited by T. W. Ogletree and published in Dallas, Texas. My attention was drawn to it by the late Professor W. S. Morris, of Lakehead University, Ontario. McCann is the author of *Christian Realism and Liberation Theology: Practical Theologies in Creative Conflict*, New York 1981, which is largely concerned with Reinhold Niebuhr, and to which reference is made later.
4. *The Church and the Bomb : Nuclear Weapons and Christian Conscience*, 1982.
5. W. A. Visser 't Hooft and J. H. Oldham, *The Church and its Function in Society*.
6. Ibid., pp. 209ff.
7. *Gaudium et Spes*, par. 43.
8. *Malvern 1941 : The Life of the Church and the Order of Society*.
9. *God's Will in our Time*, p. 32. John Baillie was the Convenor.
10. In Britain the title is *Christian Social Action*, 1954. It is an important and neglected book.
11. *The Church and the Disorder of Society*, p. 28, n. 1.
12. Paul Ramsey, *Basic Christian Ethics*, 1953.
13. Ibid., p. 350. In *Who Speaks for the Churches?*, Edinburgh 1969, he quotes with approval a Presidential Address by John Bennett to the American Society of Christian Ethics in 1961 on 'Principles and Contexts', in which he said 'The corporate teaching of the Church on controversial social issues is seldom more specific than the projection of so-called "middle axioms" (p. 14). But Ramsey does not really like the concept (see p. 169, n. 4); see also n. 39 below.
14. *Ethics in a Christian context*, 1963, p. 152.
15. 'The Logic of Moral Arguments' in *Towards a Discipline of*

Social Ethics: Essays in Honour of Walter George Muelder ed Paul Deats, Boston 1972.

16. Based on R. M. Hare, *The Language of Morals*, 1952, and subsequent books.

17. G. Gutierrez, *A Theology of Liberation*, 1973.

18. John 15.12.

19. 'Christian Ethics in America' in *Christian Ethics and the Community*, Philadelphia 1971.

20. A term from Stephen Toulmin, *Human Understanding: The Collective Use and Evolution of Concepts*, Princeton, New Jersey 1972.

21. Dennis McCann, art. cit., p. 86 (see n. 3 above).

22. Ibid., pp. 93–103.

23. *Christian Social Ethics in a Revolutionary Age*, Uppsala 1973, p. 104.

24. In *Christianity and Social Order*, chapter 5.

25. Particularly in the book with that title, 1931.

26. *Prophecy and Praxis*, p. 129.

27. Lest one should be too optimistic on this point we can reflect that the Christian church has always held that a special concern for the poor is involved in the gospel. It has never been denied. But the history of the various ways in which this radical imperative has been 'spiritualized', and remediable actions with respect to the social state of the poor evaded, is a dismal one.

28. See chapter 3.

29. *Transnational Corporations: Confronting the Issues*, 1983.

30. The report was printed in *The Ecumenical Review*, Vol 25, No 4, October 1973.

31. *The Challenge of War and Peace: God's Promise and our Response* (The US Bishops' Pastoral Letter on War and Peace in the Nuclear Age), 1983.

32. J. H. Newman, *On Consulting the Faithful in Matters of Doctrine* ed with introduction by J. Coulson, 1961.

33. The strong point of the Report is the plausibility of its case that (1) the progress of technological innovation has markedly increased the accuracy of nuclear weapons and also made small, precise ones both possible and cheap, (2) the use of these would almost certainly lead to escalation and an all-out nuclear war, and that therefore (3) the so-called nuclear balance which has kept the peace among the militarily nuclear powers for a generation has become radically de-stabilized. If it had kept to the middle level it might well have clarified the issues of public debate better than by producing its proposals for staged unilateral nuclear disarmament by the UK. This has produced a polarized unilateral versus multi-lateral discussion in the church, which has echoed rather than

clarified public discussion. The many nuclear armament supporters who argue that what has kept the peace for more than a generation must be maintained and developed have not been challenged by the strong points of the middle level case of the Report.

34. 1971, par. 4.

35. In a chapter 'What is Distinctive in Christian Social Theology?' in *Christians and the Future of Social Democracy* ed M. H. Taylor, 1982.

36. Ibid., p. 41.

37. See the discussion in chapters 5 and 6.

38. Differences lie chiefly where questions of population are involved, where anything official from Rome is tied to *Humanae Vitae*, even if unofficially things are different.

39. In *Who Speaks for the Church?* His action-orientated principles do not go as far as middle axioms. Because of his suspicion of experts, and his awareness of the uncertainties of empirical evidence, he wants the churches to refrain from making any empirical judgments, leaving these to 'the magistrates'. Only Christians as individuals can operate at the empirical level. In my view this is too much of a 'Two Realms' doctrine, making too sharp a distinction between the realms. Also, it ignores the institutional aspects and interests of the church.

40. See *Open Thy Mouth for the Dumb!; The German Evangelical Church and the Jews 1879–1950*, Richard Gutteridge 1976.

41. The terms come from Dietrich Bonhoeffer's *Ethics*, ET 1955; see pp. 103–110 of the third (rearranged) impression 1978.

42. The difference between those who are pacifist 'on principle' and the rest cannot be resolved. Those who expect to make a moral decision on principle alone on any one isuse cannot work on a middle axiom basis because that involves a consequentialist element. If they think all moral decisions are made in this way they cannot work on it at all.

43. See the discussion in chapter 6, section 3.

44. Such as, for example, Christian Concern for South Africa, or Church Action on Poverty.

Supplementary Bibliography

The place of publication is London unless otherwise stated.
Ackerman, B., *Social Justice in the Liberal State*, New Haven 1980
Anderson, P., *Considerations on Western Marxism*, 1976
Atkinson, A. B., *Unequal Shares*, 1974
Avila, R., *Worship and Politics*, New York 1981
Baum, G., *Religion and Alienation*, 1975
Beckmann, D. M., *Where Faith and Economics Meet*, Minneapolis 1981
Bell, D. (ed), *The Radical Right*, New York 1964
——, *The Coming Post-Industrial Society*, 1974
Benne, R., *The Ethics of Democratic Capitalism*, Philadelphia 1981
Berger, P., *The Homeless Mind*, New York 1974
Bornkamm, H., *Luther's Doctrine of the Two Kingdoms*, ET Philadelphia 1966
Brown, R. A. C., *The Social Psychology of Industry*, 1954
Coats, A. W., *The Classical Economists and Economic Policy*, 1971
Comblin, José, *The Church and the National Security State*, New York 1979
Crosby, M., *Spirituality of the Beatitudes: Matthew's Challenge for First-World Christians*, New York 1981
Davies, J. G., *Christians, Politics and Violent Revolution*, 1976
Davis, C., *Theology and Political Society*, 1980
Donnison, D. V., *The Politics of Poverty*, 1982
Dooyeweerd, H., *The Christian Idea of the State*, New Jersey 1968
Dussel, E., *Ethics and the Theology of Liberation*, New York 1978
Field, F., *Inequality in Britain: Freedom, Welfare and the State*, 1981
Fierro, A., *The Militant Gospel*, 1977
Freire, P., *Pedagogy of the Oppressed*, 1972
Glennerster, H. (ed), *The Future of the Welfare State*, 1983
Gottwald, N. K., *All the Kingdoms of the Earth*, New York 1964
Gough, I., *The Political Economy of the Welfare State*, 1979
Grand, Julian le, *The Strategy of Equality: Redistribution and the Social Services*, 1982
Griffiths, B., *Morality and the Market Place*, 1982
Hare, R. M., *Moral Thinking: its Levels, Methods and Point*, 1981
Hauerwas, S., *A Community of Character: Toward a Constructive Christian Social Ethic*, Indianapolis 1981
Hayek, F. A. von, *Law, Legislation and Liberty*
    Vol 1, *Rules and Order*, 1973
    Vol 2, *The Mirage of Social Justice*, 1976
    Vol 3, *The Political Order of a Free People*, 1979
Heilbroner, R. L., *An Enquiry into the Human Prospect*, New York 1974
Hill, D., *New Testament Prophecy*, 1979

Holland, H. S., *A Bundle of Memories*, 1915
Hunt, E. K., & Schwartz, J. G., *A Critique of Economic Theory*, 1972
Hutchison, T. W., *On Revolution and Progress in Economic Knowledge*, 1979
Kee, A. (ed), *The Scope of Political Theology*, 1978
Kirk, J. A., *Theology Encounters Revolution*, 1980
Knight, F. H., *The Ethics of Competition and Other Essays*, 1935
Kristol, I., & Novak, M. (eds), *Capitalism and Socialism: a Theological Enquiry*, Washington 1979
Leech, K., *The Social God*, 1981
Lefever, E., *Amsterdam to Nairobi: The World Council of Churches and the Third World*, Washington 1979
Lindblom, J., *Prophecy in Ancient Israel*, 1962
Lipsey, D., & Leonard, D. (eds), *The Social Agenda: Crosland's Legacy*, 1981
Little, I. M. D., *A Critique of Welfare Economics*, 1950
Lucas, J. R., *On Justice*, 1980
Lyttleton, E., *The Mind and Character of Henry Scott Holland*, 1926
Mahan, B., & Richesin, L. D., *The Challenge of Liberation Theology: a First World Response*, New York 1981
Maritain, J., *The Rights of Man and Natural Law*, 1944
Meadows, D. H., Randers, J., & Behrens, W. W., *The Limits to Growth*, 1972
Merton, T., *Contemplation in a World of Action*, 1971
Metz, J. B., *Faith in History and Society: Towards a Fundamental Practical Theology*, 1980
Mott, S. C., *Biblical Ethics and Social Change*, New York 1982
Munby, D. L., *God and the Rich Society*, 1961
Nankivell, O., *All Good Gifts: a Christian View of the Affluent Society*, 1978
Niebuhr, Reinhold, *The Children of Light and the Children of Darkness*, 1944
Novak, M., *The Spirit of Democratic Capitalism*, New York 1982
Nove, A., & Nuti, D. M., *The Economics of Socialism*, 1972
Olson, M., *The Rise and Decline of Nations: Economic Growth, Stagnation and Social Rigidities*, New Haven 1982
Paget, S., *Henry Scott Holland: Memoirs and Letters*, 1921
Preston, R. H., *Explorations in Theology – 9*, 1981
Quinton, A., *The Politics of Imperfection*, 1978
Reardon, B. M. G., *Henry Scott Holland: a Selection from his Writings*, 1962
Report to the President, *The Global 2,000*, Washington 1980
Schumacher, E. F., *Small is Beautiful: A Study of Economics as if People Mattered*, 1973
Sider, R. (ed), *Life Style in the Eighties: an Evangelical Commitment to Simple Life Style*, 1981
——, *Evangelicals and Development: Towards a Theology of Social Change*, 1981

Sleeman, J. F., *Economic Problems: a Christian Approach*, 1953
——, *The Welfare State*, 1973
——, *Economic Crisis: a Christian Perspective*, 1976
Soloway, R. A., *Prelates and People: Ecclesiastical Social Thought in England 1783–1832*, 1969
Stamp, J., *Motive and Method in a Christian Order*, 1936
——, *Christianity and Economics*, 1939
Stonier, T., *The Wealth of Information: A Profile of the Post-Industrial Economy*, 1983
Tawney, R. H., *Equality*, ³1938
Thurow, L., *The Zero-Sum Society*, 1980
Vincent, J. J., *Starting all over Again*, Geneva 1981
Ward, A. D. (ed), *Goals of Economic Life*, New York 1953
Waterman, C., *Basic Forms of Prophetic Speech*, 1967
Wilson, R. R., *Prophecy in Ancient Israel*, Philadelphia 1980
Yoder, J. H., *The Politics of Jesus: Vicit Agnus Noster*, Grand Rapids 1972

Index of Names